T0198461

YOUSUF HAMID

HOW TO
TE↑CH
ECON↑OMICS

First published 2022

by John Catt Educational Ltd,
15 Riduna Park, Station Road,
Melton, Woodbridge IP12 1QT

Tel: +44 (0) 1394 389850
Fax: +44 (0) 1394 386893
Email: enquiries@johncatt.com
Website: www.johncatt.com

© **Yousuf Hamid 2022**

No part of this publication may be reproduced, stored
in a retrieval system, transmitted in any form or by
any means, electronic, mechanical, photocopying,
recording, or otherwise, without the prior permission
of the publishers.

Opinions expressed in this publication are those
of the contributors and are not necessarily those
of the publishers or the editors. We cannot accept
responsibility for any errors or omissions.

ISBN: 978 1 915261 05 2

Set and designed by John Catt Educational Limited

For Lilja and Lottie – colleagues and life-savers

CONTENTS

↑ INTRODUCTION

Teaching economics is perhaps the greatest thing I have done for anyone in my life. The opportunity to explain how economics can unlock the mysteries of the world and lift the blindfold to show the world as it really is, is a privilege. It is only in teaching the subject that I've fully been able to appreciate the meaning of Keynes' famous quote that 'practical men who believe themselves to be quite exempt from any intellectual influence, are usually the slaves of some defunct economist.' Yet, as the no-less profound uncle Ben in *Spiderman* says, 'with great power comes great responsibility.'

Teaching is, indeed, a great responsibility and most teachers have the support of large departments, blogs from practising teachers, shared resources online, books from subject experts and academic research. These help bridge the gap between research from cognitive science and its application in the classroom for particular subjects.

Unfortunately, in economics this is rarely the case. Many of us work by ourselves or with one colleague. While this keeps department meetings rather brief, it also limits our opportunities for collaboration. Similarly, there is not much written about how to apply research to teaching economics, and only a relatively small community of teachers sharing resources and tips online.

While there has been an explosion in recent years of teachers discussing how to interpret research in the classroom and much of it is excellent, the challenge has always been the subject specificity of economics. With everything I read, I have to ask myself: how does this apply to economics?

The purpose of this book is to answer that question. It looks at the major research on how our brains work and applies that specifically to the economics classroom. While we will look at exactly what research says about different aspects of teaching, this book is unashamedly practical, and focused on exactly what this entails for economics teachers.

Many of the lessons this book is based on have come from trial and error: I read some research and attempted to integrate it into my teaching. Occasionally it went very well, sometimes it was okay, and, truthfully, most of the time it was an unmitigated disaster. Slowly, I discovered what worked well and what didn't for our subject. I hope these pages can save you some of that upheaval.

We will look at retrieval practice, cognitive load theory and assessment – all of which can improve pupils' learning. I hope to show what a difference they can make to teaching our wonderful subject, and that you will find ways to tweak your practice as a result.

We will also look at curriculum. A hot topic since the changes made to the Ofsted inspection framework in 2019, it can often feel less relevant for a subject without key stage 3. I hope to demonstrate that hard thinking and challenging discussions about curriculum are, in fact, not only relevant but absolutely necessary to teaching economics well.

Lastly, we will look at writing. Much of the academic and teacher literature around this, unsurprisingly, relates to English and history. Yet writing in economics is quite unique. No other subject requires the same blend of analytical reasoning, application from an extract, use of diagrams and quantitative analysis, or evaluative decision making about contemporary issues. In this section, I hope to explain how to ensure pupils are able to analyse, apply and evaluate economic concepts in order to excel, not just in exams, but in their broader understanding of economics.

Thank you for taking the time to read this. At a time when workload is at a historical high and pressure mounts to ensure our students catch up from the effects of the pandemic, I know that investing in reading can feel superfluous or indulgent. To that end, every page that follows is designed to do two things: help you to maximise the impact of your teaching, and save you time by cutting out ineffective methods and practices.

Teaching economics brings me great professional and personal joy, and I hope that sharing the lessons I've learned helps bring some of that joy to you.

COGNITIVE LOAD THEORY

Ever since Dylan Wiliam tweeted in 2017 about 'the single most important thing for a teacher to know', there has been huge interest in what John Sweller's cognitive load theory (CLT) is and how it can be applied in the classroom.

While the dense academic literature around CLT can initially appear confusing, the underlying purpose of the theory is to provide the framework to improve teacher instruction and thereby ensure pupils are able to remember more of what we teach them. As Sweller himself put it, 'the ultimate aim of cognitive load theory is to provide instructional effects leading to instructional recommendations' (Sweller, 2016).

WHAT THE RESEARCH SAYS

Our memory system

CLT splits our memory system into three components: environment, working memory and long-term memory.

The environment consists of everything that is not within our heads. It could be knowledge on the internet, what a pupil sitting in the front row says, a book *etc*. It is an almost unlimited reservoir of information.

Long-term memory is where we store all of our memories. This can be everything from the time your partner told you he loved you (what is referred to as episodic knowledge), the lyrics to every Arctic Monkeys song (factual or semantic knowledge), or the memory of processes like how to tie a knot or draw an externalities diagram (procedural knowledge). Just as the environment is an unlimited external source of information, your long-term memory (as far as researchers are currently aware) is an unlimited internal source of information.

So, if our long-term memory is potentially unlimited, our pupils should be able to store everything said by every economist who has ever lived. Much like my family holidays from Glasgow to Blackpool as a child, the journey is as much a part of the adventure as the destination. And just like those holidays, the issue is that in order for knowledge to arrive into our long-term memory, it needs to go through a bottleneck: our working memory, the M6 of our memory system.

Working memory is where our thinking takes place. In order to go from the unlimited external knowledge of our environment and arrive at the unlimited internal capacity of our long-term memory, information needs to go through our working memory. The big difference between working memory and the other two components of the system is capacity. Our working memory is limited, and while researchers dispute the exact number, it is thought broadly to be able to hold between four and seven bits of information before it becomes overloaded (Cowan, 2001).

Imagine our pupil sat in her economics class listening to her teacher explain what price elasticity of demand is. She is obtaining knowledge from her environment (the teacher), but for it to enter her long-term memory she is going to have to think about this new knowledge using her very limited working memory first. There, she will have to connect the new term to prior knowledge (what demand is; why quantity demanded increases when the price of a good decreases; what is meant by sensitivity to demand) in order to make sense of all its implications (the formula for the price elasticity of demand; what different values of price elasticity of demand mean; the implications for firms setting prices and governments setting taxes; how this can be drawn in a diagram; and the relationship between elasticity of demand and revenue).

We are very quickly reaching well beyond the four to seven pieces of information our pupil's working memory is able to process, and so she finds herself quickly over-loaded. Oliver Lovell described cognitive load as 'anything that takes up working memory capacity' (2020). And avoiding overload is why much of the discussion around CLT centres around 'chunking' information.

As Rosenshine said in his seminal 2012 paper on effective instruction, the key is to 'present new material in small steps'. This is especially important in teaching as new information takes up more working memory capacity than familiar information. When our pupil draws a demand curve for the first time, this takes up a lot of working memory capacity (and by the number of examination papers I have marked with incorrect labelling of axes, perhaps not enough thinking has gone into this!). But as she becomes more experienced at drawing these and the procedural knowledge of drawing a demand curve enters her long-term memory, drawing the curve takes up less of her working memory. It has become automated.

So, as long as we chunk our explanation of elasticities so that there are no more than four to seven pieces of new information at any one time, our pupil will be able to fully process the concept and ensure it enters her long-term memory, right? Sadly, that is not all that is occupying the working memory of our pupil. She is also trying to read the teacher's PowerPoint slide while he is speaking. She is laughing at the 'funny' gif her teacher put on that slide. She is still thinking about the argument she had with her friend at lunch. She is trying to work out the right format to complete a worksheet and when she is to stick it into her exercise book. With all of this in her working memory, there is almost no capacity left for understanding what price elasticity of demand is and how its application impacts so many facets of her life.

Intrinsic and extraneous load

While CLT shows what takes up working memory, not all cognitive load is equal. The subject of our lesson today is price elasticity of demand. This core knowledge is what CLT theorists refer to as *intrinsic load* and it is exactly what we want our pupils to be thinking about. But this intrinsic load is competing with *extraneous load*. Much of this actually comes from the manner and structure of instruction (sometimes referred to as the 'froth' around instruction) – the things that might make teaching exciting for us but are not directly related to the content that we want pupils to understand.

The important thing to remember is that the very limited capacity of our working memory is the total sum of both intrinsic and extraneous load. Think of pouring water and orange juice into a glass. It doesn't matter how much of each liquid you pour in, when the glass is full there is simply no more space for anything else to enter it.

Basically, extraneous load is taking up valuable working memory capacity that we want our pupils to use on the intrinsic load of the content we are teaching. It is why the golden rule of CLT is to reduce extraneous load and to optimise intrinsic load (Lovell, 2020).

We will shortly be looking at ways to optimise intrinsic load in economics, but first of all, let's review a few simple ways research tells us we can reduce extraneous load.

The redundancy effect
The most obvious is the redundancy effect. This states that extraneous load is often taken up by redundant information and can therefore be reduced by minimising that redundant information and avoiding replication of necessary information. Redundant information can be seen when there are unnecessary images or icons on a worksheet that are not relevant to the task. It can also be heard when a teacher reads text that pupils can read for themselves. It can be experienced when a task (or 'game') requires pupils to use much of their thinking capacity on information that is not related to the content being taught (like rules, for example). It can even be when a teacher goes off on a tangent about a related point which, interesting as it might be for all involved, is superfluous to the aim of the lesson.

The point about images is often a contentious one, especially as interest in dual coding continues to grow. The important distinction to make here is that images can be considered redundant if they show the same information as is already explained verbally or in writing. A quick way to reduce extraneous load is therefore to go through your slides and classroom materials and, for each image ask: 'Does this explain content I want my pupils to understand that has not already been explained?' If not, remove it!

The split-attention effect
The second way to reduce extraneous load relates to the split-attention effect. If two or more related pieces of information are presented too close

together or too far apart, this places additional extraneous load on working memory by forcing pupils to integrate the information themselves instead of giving their full capacity over to engaging with the intrinsic load of the lesson at hand. Take, for example, a slide containing a diagram side-by-side with bullet points explaining what a 'supernormal profit' is. The cognitive effort of understanding the text in relation to the diagram places a considerable (and unproductive) load on pupils' working memory.

The split-attention effect applies not only to the distance between items in terms of space, but also in terms of time. Every teacher has had the experience of giving pupils multiple instructions before a task and then being surprised when they are unable to follow them when the time comes to put them into action. The issue is not pupils deliberately ignoring instructions (well, maybe sometimes!) but that the time that has elapsed since the instruction makes it harder for pupils to remember. It simply requires more cognitive effort to remember what the instruction was.

Interestingly, Sweller and Chandler (1994) conducted research that showed pupils were more able to accurately fill out spreadsheets after reading a high-quality instruction manual than alternating between a manual and using a computer to practice. Their study neatly demonstrated the perils of the split-attention impact on valuable working memory capacity.

At this point, the implication might seem that we should integrate all images and text together, so as to avoid the split-attention effect. However, it is important not to fall into the trap of ignoring the redundancy effect mentioned earlier. John Sweller put this very succinctly: 'If a learner can't understand a diagram and text without considering them both then they should be physically integrated. If the text re-describes the diagram, it should be removed as it forces learners to read redundant text' (Lovell, 2020).

The transient information effect
To understand the third way to reduce extraneous load, let's go back to our pupil trying to learn about price elasticity of demand. Imagine she is reading a slide providing this key concept's definition. The teacher's presentation moves on to a slide showing diagrams with different gradients of demand curves and explaining how these vary based on elasticity. Our pupil now must remember the definition on the previous slide while also

trying to understand how it relates to these diagrams. Much of her working memory is spent on the challenge of remembering the definition, which is now gone from the screen, instead of how this relates to the steepness of demand curves.

This is the transient information effect. Put simply, it means that when information disappears, pupils need to hold it in their working memory in order to use it, essentially converting intrinsic load into extraneous load.

There are numerous quick wins to try to minimise this negative effect. It is possible to incorporate previous information on slides. In the example above, a reminder of the definition of price elasticity of demand could be incorporated on the slide that shows the different demand curves, allowing our pupil to focus all her cognitive energy on understanding the diagram. However, this should only be provided at the point when it is needed, otherwise the large amount of information can lead to the redundancy effect discussed above. Similarly, providing a printout of slides can reduce the transient information effect but in this case (as with booklets, which we will look at below), it's important to ensure pupils only look at the relevant information at the right time to avoid introducing redundant information.

It is common to encounter the transient information effect when showing pupils videos or engaging in class discussions, because the points they introduce are immediately gone. This can be ameliorated by regularly pausing the discussion or video and modelling note-taking on the board. This allows pupils to easily capture relevant information while continuing to partake in the discussion.

We will continue to refer to CLT as we go through this chapter and throughout this book as it is relevant to numerous aspects of teaching. For the moment, however, the important point to understand is that while the environment and long-term memory are potentially unlimited, working memory is a bottleneck, and all new information must get through to become secure knowledge. To do this effectively, we need to reduce extraneous load and to optimise intrinsic load.

So far, we have looked at how to reduce extraneous load because the methods for doing so are broadly generic. But optimising intrinsic load is where things get specific, so let's get into the nitty gritty of applying CLT in the economics classroom.

HOW TO OPTIMISE ECONOMICS TEACHING

Explaining material in small steps

As economics teachers, the first step to optimising intrinsic load is to carefully consider the sequence of our explanations. Getting this right requires us to understand what discrete pieces of knowledge we need our pupils to understand for the next concept they encounter to make sense. Then, there need to be opportunities for pupils to think about and work with this knowledge before moving onto the next piece, to avoid overloading their working memories.

The biggest challenge to 'chunking' material like this and explaining it in small steps is a form of cognitive bias called 'the curse of knowledge.' In 1990, a Stanford University psychology graduate conducted an experiment where participants would tap a well-known song and others would have to guess it (Newton, 1990). The participants estimated that around 50 per cent of people would correctly guess the song. In reality, it was 3.5 per cent. Because the participant knew the song she was tapping, she assumed others would guess it too. So it is with teaching. Because we know the content so well, it can be difficult to appreciate how much a concept needs to be broken down to be understood by the novice learner.

Explaining externalities

Externalities is a microeconomic concept that pupils often find challenging. When I teach negative consumption externality for the first time, I break down the concept into incredibly granular steps, going as far as I can without sacrificing the overall meaning of the concept.

The steps that explain are:

1. What a transaction is.
2. What benefits and costs consumers incur in a transaction.
3. What benefits and costs producers incur in a transaction.
4. What a third party to a transaction means.
5. How consuming a good can incur a cost to a third party.

6. The concept of external costs.

7. Why consumers do not consider external costs when choosing how much to consume.

8. Why this leads to over-consumption.

9. Why this is an inefficient allocation of resources.

10. The meaning of a welfare loss.

11. The concept of marginal private and marginal social costs and benefits.

12. How this is shown in a diagram.

So, a concept which to an economics teacher seems fairly simple actually requires 12 different steps that need to be understood – far more than could be understood in one go by a pupil without overloading their working memory. After each of these small steps, pupils must have a chance to answer several questions to ensure they understand it. This is the only way to ease the passage of the new information from the environment into their long-term memory.

But that's not enough. With each step, we must also ask questions about all the previous steps so that pupils are able to start putting the pieces together. This is sometimes referred to as 'snowballing' questions: asking about all prior steps, as well as the step they have just learned. When I have explained what a third party to a transaction is, as well as checking their knowledge and understanding of the new term, I also ask them what a transaction is, the two parties to a transaction and the benefits and costs of a transaction to consumers and firms. By the time they get to step 12, they have been asked about each step so many times that they start to build fluency. Each step starts to become automated, optimising intrinsic load.

Monopolistic Competition
Another commonly misunderstood topic is market structures. It can be a tricky one to break down into component parts as so much of it revolves around drawing diagrams. The trick is often to be able to explain why each curve is the shape it is, and gradually building up a diagram.

The steps I break this down into are:

1. The assumptions of monopolistic competition.

2. How this differs to perfect competition.

3. Why scarcity means that if a firm reduces its quantity, the price will increase and vice versa.

4. Why this is not the case under perfect competition.

5. Drawing a downward sloping average revenue curve based on this concept.

6. Why firms' marginal revenue differs from their average revenue.

7. Re-drawing the earlier diagram with both average and marginal revenue.

8. The incentive impact if firms make a supernormal profit.

9. Why in the long run firms make a normal profit.

10. The concept that a normal profit occurs when average cost equals average revenue.

11. A reminder that profit is maximised when marginal revenue equals marginal cost.

12. A final drawing of the monopolistic competition diagram with all curves showing.

When I am building a diagram like this, I like to draw it live. The reason for this is to build up the diagram curve by curve, explaining each step along the way to avoid the redundancy effect and keep pupils' working memory processing the new information efficiently. I also add labels when relevant to avoid the split-attention effect.

You could animate a PowerPoint to do all this, revealing each new curve when the pupils are ready for it, but I prefer to use a mini whiteboard under a visualiser. It means I can be more responsive to my classes and adapt my explanations based on those areas pupils are struggling with most.

The use of booklets

One potential problem with this method is the transient information effect. Once the diagram is removed from the screen and you have finished speaking, pupils immediately begin to exert considerable cognitive load to remember what has been said and to apply it to the task you have asked them to complete.

A way to get around this is to use topic booklets for pupils to complete. For me, these contain nothing more than short explanations and diagrams and many practice questions. This means pupils can refer to these while answering questions on each step, thereby limiting the transient information effect.

There is a danger here though. Pupils rushing ahead to different notes and explanations instead of focusing on the carefully sequenced explanations you have prepared will only increase intrinsic load and potentially cause confusion. In order to avoid this pitfall, it is necessary to have clear expectations that pupils will not look at these notes when you are explaining a concept. In *Teach Like a Champion*, Doug Lemov (2015) recommends teaching routines like SLANT for what pupils should be doing when you are speaking:

- Sit straight
- Listen
- Answer questions
- Nothing in your hand
- Track the teacher

Some economics teachers worry that this infantilises sixth form pupils, but in my experience this has not been an issue. A clear routine for listening becomes crucial to ensure booklets do not fall prey to the redundant information trap. It also scaffolds their progression towards the kind of self-discipline that will stand them in good stead for their higher education.

Avoiding shallow engagement

When I started teaching, I tried all manner of ways to make my lessons 'fun.' From inflation board games to bringing in sweets to explain opportunity cost, and even some cringe-inducing role plays to demonstrate the allocation of scarce resources. The most cursory glance at online resources will return an abundance of these types of lessons.

And the simple fact is that they impose huge extraneous load on pupils. The amount of working memory capacity that goes on the rules and procedures of the game mean there is very little capacity left for what inflation actually is! It is why tasks like creating posters or newspaper front pages about a concept are such a waste of time, too; pupils are devoting so much of their cognitive load on the aesthetics of the piece instead of the concept itself.

Daniel Willingham (2010) famously stated that 'memory is the residue of thought'. Perhaps one of the most important learning points from CLT is that pupils will remember what they have thought about.

So, every economics lesson needs to be about the economics, and nothing else. If that sounds ruthless, my experience teaches me that the joy in a classroom comes from the learning itself. The best way to ensure pupils are engaged in the classroom is to ensure they are continuing to learn more economics. The subject is such an eye-opener to the world that it is enough. There is no need to introduce artificial 'fun'. Pedagogical bells and whistles only inhibit pupils' learning.

KEY POINTS

- Pupils take information from the external environment in order to store it into their long-term memory.
- While these are both unlimited, information must first travel through pupils' (limited) working memory.
- The cognitive load upon pupils' working memory is made up of the intrinsic load of what you are teaching, and extraneous load.
- Effective and efficient teaching means optimising internal load and reducing extraneous load.
- Reducing extraneous load means stripping out redundant information, avoiding split attention by keeping related material close together in space and time, and minimising the transient information effect.
- Optimising intrinsic load means breaking complex topics down into granular steps, building in and building up diagrams and other complex processes as part of the step-by-step journey, using booklets while ensuring their use is disciplined, and keeping the subject the main (and only) thing.

REFERENCES

Cowan, N. (2001) 'The Magical Number 4 in Short-Term Memory: A Reconsideration of Mental Storage Capacity', *The Behavioral and brain sciences.* 24, pp. 87-114.

Lemov, D. (2015) *Teach Like a Champion 2.0 62 techniques that put students on the path to college.* San Francisco: Jossey-Bass.

Lovell, O. (2020) *Sweller's Cognitive Load Theory in Action.* 1st ed. Woodbridge: John Catt Educational.

Newton, E. L. (1990) *The rocky road from actions to intentions* (PhD diss). Stanford University [online]. Available at https://creatorsvancouver.com/wp-content/uploads/2016/06/rocky-road-from-actions-to-intentions.pdf (Accessed 10/02/2022).

Rosenshine, B. (2012) 'Principles of instruction: Research-based strategies that all teachers should know', *American Educator.* 36, pp. 12-39.

Sweller, J. (2016, February 10) 'Story of a Research Program.' In Tobias, S., Fletcher, J. D. and Berliner, D. C. (Series eds.) Acquired Wisdom Series. *Education Review.* 23 (12).

Sweller, J., & Chandler, P. (1994) 'Why some material is difficult to learn', *Cognition and Instruction,* 12, pp. 185–233.

Wiliam, D. (2017) [Twitter] January 26. Available at: https://twitter.com/dylanwiliam/status/824682504602943489?s=20&t=JQd76vv2SvhCS0nlc2Z1Kw (Accessed: 05/02/2021).

Willingham, D. (2010) *Why Don't Students Like School? A cognitive scientist answers questions about how the mind works and what it means for the classroom.* San Francisco: Jossey Bass.

↑ RETRIEVAL PRACTICE

I vividly remember, in my first year of teaching, asking my year 12 pupils to define what opportunity cost was. For all the challenges of that NQT year, that lesson offered a rare glimmer of light. Everyone understood what opportunity cost was and all were able to apply it in different settings. Fast forward a month and I was certain that pupils would be able to quickly explain it to me so we could move on with the day's lesson.

Only a lifetime following the Scottish national football team can prepare you for the disappointment I felt as I looked at rows of blank faces instead, staring back at me as though I was speaking a different language. I couldn't comprehend how my pupils couldn't even begin to answer a question I thought they had fluently understood only a matter of weeks before. The thorny issue of how to get pupils to remember what they have been taught has vexed teachers since time immemorial. Fortunately, there is a growing body of research to help teachers ensure what we impart to our pupils stays with them.

WHAT THE RESEARCH SAYS

Practice makes perfect

Retrieval practice is the process by which pupils are supported to remember information they have previously been taught with little or no notes to help them. Just as practising playing the guitar makes you a better guitar player, the process of trying to remember information actually strengthens your memory of that information. As Robert Bjork states, 'using your memory shapes your memory' (2012).

There is a common misconception with retrieval practice that it is about pupils remembering information because they have discovered knowledge for themselves rather than being explicitly taught by an expert. Overwhelming empirical evidence now shows us that minimal guided instruction does not work for novice learners (Kirschner, Sweller and Clark, 2006). Instead, retrieval practice is about remembering information that has already been taught.

This links back to our discussion of CLT in chapter one. When information goes from the teacher (the external environment), it is initially processed through pupils' limited short-term memory before, hopefully, entering their unlimited long-term memory. The problem is that just because it is in a pupil's long-term memory, it does not mean that it will be easy to retrieve again when needed. Just think of when you are at the cinema. You see an actor you know but you can't quite remember their name. Retrieval practice is about strengthening that retrieval strength so that pupils can recall information from their long-term memory.

David Didau spoke of this in terms of retrieval storage and retrieval strength (Didau and Rose, 2016). Retrieval storage refers to how strongly embedded information is in a pupil's long-term memory and retrieval strength is how easily it can be brought to mind when required. A simpler way of looking at this is that retrieval storage is the information that has made its way into pupils' heads (as a result of what we would traditionally consider teaching) and retrieval strength is the ease with which they can get that information back out. And the latter is where retrieval practice can be so useful.

There is now an overwhelming body of evidence that retrieval practice improves pupils' memory. In a landmark study that has since been replicated across a wide range of subjects and demographics, Henry Roediger and Jeffrey Karpicke (2006) instructed university students to read a passage about sea otters and the sun. Then, one group re-read the passage while others had to write down everything they could remember about it. After five minutes, those who had re-read did much better in a test (83%) than those who engaged in retrieval practice (71%). Crucially, however, a week later this was completely reversed. Student performance was much higher for those who had engaged in retrieval practice. This shows the method's clear effectiveness, but it gets to the crux of why some students struggle with it too: over time, they forget far less, but at first it feels harder and even potentially less effective.

There are a number of benefits of regular retrieval practice, among which the most commonly cited is to strengthen later retention. Building on Bjork's claim that using your memory can shape your memory, Cooney Horvath (2019) showed that 'every time you retrieve a memory, it becomes deeper, stronger and easier to access in the future'. An indirect yet equally important benefit of retrieval practice is that pupils can identify gaps in their knowledge when they see what questions they were unable to answer. In other words, it can aid pupils in identifying what areas they need to focus their study on.

Unfortunately, every teacher has had the experience of pupils who would prefer to re-read their notes and highlight sections rather than to test themselves. Karpicke, Butler and Roediger (2009) surveyed 177 college students and found that 57% of students' preferred method of studying was to re-read a textbook chapter. Only 18% would attempt to test themselves.

Perhaps it is not surprising that pupils choose re-reading over retrieval. It certainly requires less cognitive work, which is precisely also why it is less effective! It can also be comforting; when you re-read something, you often feel like you understand it more as you become more fluent in the reading itself. But it does little to ensure you are able to remember what you have read. As The Learning Scientists explained, 'students re-reading provides a false sense of confidence in comparison to practice testing.' (Sumeracki, Weinstein and Caviglioli, 2018).

One concern by some about retrieval practice is that it only improves the memorisation of facts and does not help with higher-order thinking. This is usually stated with reference to Bloom's taxonomy of learning, which is usually represented as a pyramid, with the ability to analyse, evaluate and create (classed as higher-order thinking) at its top. Putting concerns over this model to one side (not least that it was never intended to be a pyramid), research has shown that following retrieval practice, pupils perform better in exams in both factual and application questions. In fact, the biggest benefit from retrieval practice came in these so-called higher-order questions (Agarwal, 2019).

While most of this chapter is dedicated to how retrieval practice can improve pupils' retention of information over the long term, there are also broader benefits. According to Roediger, Putnam and Smith (2011), the top 10 are:

1. Improved learning and long-term retention of information.
2. Increased higher-order thinking and transfer of knowledge.
3. Identification of gaps in knowledge, improving formative assessment.
4. Increased metacognition and awareness of own learning.
5. Increased engagement and attention in class.
6. Increased use of effective study strategies outside of class.
7. Increased advance preparation for class.
8. Improved mental organisation of knowledge.
9. Increased learning of related information.
10. Increased learning in the future by blocking interfering information.

Spaced practice

So, if retrieval practice has such benefits, the question then is when should we ask pupils to do it? And the answer is in a technique called spaced practice, in which 'spaced' refers to the time in between a pupil learning new information and then retrieving it. Spacing is no different to retrieval practice, but puts the onus on how often pupils are asked to retrieve information in order to make their knowledge more secure and more easily accessible when needed.

The 'forgetting curve' and the 'golden gap'

And it's not new. German psychologist Hermann Ebbinghaus first hypothesised his 'forgetting curve' in 1885, showing how quickly people forget information after being taught it and how the curve becomes less steep as people have to retrieve the information over time. It's a study that has since been replicated numerous times (Murre and Dros, 2015). There is also more recent research showing the impact of spacing retrieval. Doug Rohrer and Kelli Taylor gave one group of pupils a lot of mathematics problems to solve in one week, while another group spaced out retrieval over four weeks. Importantly, the same total amount of time was spent on the problems; the only difference was whether it was crammed. After four weeks, those who crammed saw their performance drop by more than half, whereas those who spaced their practice only saw their performance drop slightly (Rohrer and Taylor, 2006).

The key here is that teachers need to ensure pupils retrieve information from previously taught material multiple times over a prolonged period. This leads many teachers to ask what the 'golden gap' between retrieval practice sessions is, to make best use of this spacing effect. The reason why spacing is effective is that pupils have started to forget and it is the difficulty of remembering that helps cement the information in long-term memory. However, if there is such a delay that the information is totally forgotten, then spacing the practice will be ineffective. So, if cramming is not effective, and waiting 12 months is likely to be too long, what should the gap in between retrievals be? Research by Nicholas Cepeda suggests that the optimal ratio is 1:10 (Cepeda, 2008). So, for research participants to remember information for 30 days they should space retrieval every three days. In order to remember information for 200 days they should retrieve it every 20 days. Of course, we want our pupils to remember what we teach for longer than 200 days, and research on this is mixed. It seems the important thing is to regularly space retrieval practice rather than trying to be too specific about exactly how long these spaces should be. Pooja Agarwal put it very simply with her two rules of spaced practice:

- More is better
- Any is better than none

So, we know that retrieval is effective, and we know it should be spaced – even if, as Cepeda says, 'the optimally efficient gap between study sessions is not some absolute' quantity that can be recommended' (Cepeda *et al.*, 2008). And this leads us to another and potentially more important question about the 'golden gap': what is it best for pupils to do during retrieval intervals on a topic?

Interleaving

The answer takes us to our final key concept for understanding and improving long-term memory: interleaving. Interleaving is the process of mixing things up during spacing. Research has shown that simply rearranging the order of retrieval opportunities can double student learning (Rohrer, 2012). Think of four topics to be taught (A, B, C and D). A traditional approach would be blocked practice so pupils learn and practice one at a time, which could look like this: AAAA-BBBB-CCCC-DDDD. An interleaved approach means pupils complete tasks on different topics as they progress through the learning sequence, and have to work out for themselves what the best strategy to solve an interleaved problem is. So interleaved practice might look like this: ABCDDABCCADBABCD.

Much of the research around interleaving has related to mathematics classrooms, but we will shortly look at how this can be used within economics. The key to presenting topics side-by-side is that pupils need to be able to discriminate between them. This means that there is a need to mix up similar topics. A useful analogy is that of a fruit salad. While you may put oranges and strawberries in a fruit salad, you are unlikely to include tomatoes. It is the same with interleaving; teachers need to mix up similar topics so that pupils struggle when considering the best approach to answer the question – but crucially have the tools and information required for the job. Interleaving is particularly effective in the middle of a scheme of work. While many remember what was learned at the start and end of a topic, forcing pupils to discriminate between topics can be particularly effective in ensuring they remember content midway through a term. Sometimes interleaving and spacing sound like they are the same thing, but they are subtly different. Spacing is how we spread content over a period of time, and interleaving is what happens in the intervals.

So, to recap: through regular retrieval practice, we are able to help pupils with long-term recall of information they have been taught without the use of aids or prompts. This strategy is more effective when it is spaced out, so that pupils retrieve the same information numerous times over a prolonged period of time. And for maximum impact, content should be interleaved so that pupils are discriminating between topics. But how can these be used in the economics classroom?

HOW TO OPTIMISE ECONOMICS LEARNING

The do-now quiz

A common way to implement retrieval practice into a lesson is to start with a quiz. In order for this to be true retrieval practice, pupils should not have notes or aides to hand, so that they are having to try to retrieve from their long-term memory. While the act of simply retrieving is itself useful, pupils should receive feedback on correct answers in order to maximise the effect. There is no need to mark these, as quizzes should appear low-stakes to pupils to be most effective. A mixture of telling pupils answers and cold-calling pupils is an excellent way to gain information about gaps in their knowledge.

A quiz can also optimise the spacing effect if questions test pupils on content that they have learned previously. In a six-question quiz, I will typically include two questions on content from the previous lesson, two on content from a week ago, and two questions on content from longer ago. As discussed above, there is no need to be overly scientific about how long ago you quizzed a particular topic. The important thing is that retrieval is spaced, rather than worrying about exactly when an item was last retrieved.

However, the previously taught content to assess in the do-now quiz largely chooses itself. This is because the often-forgotten purpose of a retrieval quiz at the start of a lesson is to ensure pupils have the prerequisite knowledge to access the new content they are about to encounter. As you go through the curriculum, pupils are expanding their schemas relating to the subject and attaching new knowledge to what they already know about it. In almost every lesson, we are relying on pupils remembering certain concepts they have been taught, and the do-now quiz ensures the teacher can fill any gaps and correct any misconceptions before moving forward.

This is true of every topic in economics, but some examples of key prerequisite knowledge I ensure to include in my do-now quizzes include:

- The economic problem of scarcity when teaching opportunity cost.
- Why demand responds to price changes when teaching a shift in a demand curve.

- Price elasticity and why demand responds to real incomes when teaching income elasticity of demand.
- The incentive function of the price mechanism and how price impacts supply and demand when teaching minimum price.
- Perfect competition, monopolies and supernormal profits when teaching oligopoly.
- Micro demand and the difference between capital and consumer goods when teaching aggregate demand.
- The long-run aggregate supply curve and the impact of low consumer confidence on aggregate demand when teaching the Keynesian supply curve.

Spaced retrieval at other times

The problem with a do-now quiz is that time constraints impose a limit on how many questions can be set. As the year progresses and the amount of content you wish pupils to regularly retrieve increases, it becomes impossible to fit this into a quiz (especially if there is only space for two or three questions about prior content in your quiz). I recently wrote a list of quiz questions about everything I wanted my pupils to know securely on the topic of microeconomics for A-level. There were 872 of them. If I wanted to quiz pupils on these six times over the year, I would need to find time to ask them 5,232 questions. And this is before we even look at macroeconomics!

Given the impossibility of the task, the most useful form of retrieval practice is often done as homework. Online platforms like Google Forms, Quizlet or Carousel Learning are very effective at randomly generating quizzes using questions you input from a wide variety of topics to utilise the spacing effect. These also have the benefit of allowing pupils to self-mark, so can be a time-efficient way to set homework. Around 70 per cent of the homework I set classes is retrieval-based, with the remainder being extended writing from data response questions.

One word of warning though: this relies on building the right culture with your class. As we have seen, retrieval is hard work for pupils and is often not their preferred method of studying. When pupils are at home, there is no way of knowing if they are actually trying to retrieve information from their memory or just looking at notes. For this to be effective, it is crucial that pupils understand the merit of retrieval so that they engage with the work in good faith. If your school has a policy of supervised independent study, then it might be worth discussing with the supervisor your expectation of no books or notes while economics homework is being completed.

A lot of teachers also ask pupils to complete end-of-topic tests. While these can be effective forms of retrieval, it is important to consider the spacing effect. It may be more effective to mix questions up from different topics that have been taught previously than to focus the test exclusively on mastery of the topic that has just been learned. There is certain information we know pupils must know like the back of their hands, and these are worth quizzing more. For example, I regularly quiz pupils on formulas for elasticities and definitions of key terms as their recall of these needs to reach complete automaticity by the end of the course.

Retrieval can also form part of your questioning as a teacher. When you are teaching about subsidies, you can say 'why would higher profits impact the supply curve again, John?' As long as you are cold calling rather than relying on hands up, and there is an appropriate pause between the question and the name, all pupils are still engaging in retrieval practice. As with homework, this will depend on having a culture where all pupils believe they could be asked a question and understand they have to participate in questioning – what Doug Lemov calls 'no opt out'.

Chains of reasoning
In great part, economics assessment objectives require pupils to demonstrate logical chains of reasoning. This is often about causal processes, and it is what paragraphs in economics essays are built around. So a pupil should be able to explain why an indirect tax leads to lower profits, how this impacts supply, why this impacts price and consumer demand, why this reduces output and why this can stop a market failure of over-production and reduce a social welfare loss. Every step in that chain needs to be understood in order for the paragraph to make sense.

One of my favourite types of retrieval practice is to give pupils a table with a chain of reasoning where some boxes are blank, so that pupils have to remember the missing links. When these are at the start or end of a chain, they are relatively straightforward. But retrieving a 'middle link' is more challenging. Practising in this way has the additional benefit of checking whether pupils really understand a particular topic rather than simply remember disconnected facts. And that's particularly useful information to build feedback on.

Discriminating between topics

As we have discussed, interleaving is most effective when pupils are having to discriminate between topics, so they have to identify the best solution for a problem. While much of the research for this is in maths and science classrooms, economics contains so many topics that appear superficially similar but are subtly different. These nuances make the subject a goldmine for interleaved questions.

Some examples of these in my classroom include:

- Giving pupils a range of scenarios and asking them to determine if they will influence price, income, or cross-elasticity of demand. For example: 'An alcoholic drink has high brand loyalty and is considered addictive. How will this influence elasticity of demand?'
- Pupils often get the factors influencing demand for labour and demand for a good confused. As above, giving pupils a range of factors and asking them to determine if this impacts demand for the good or the labour market can be effective. Using mini whiteboards for such activities makes for a rapid way to gather information and give immediate feedback on any misconceptions.
- If pupils can explain the differences between direct, indirect, progressive, regressive and proportional taxes, ask them to give examples of each. Finally, providing some examples of each and asking them to categorise which type of tax they are adds another level of challenge. I have never known a pupil to be able to get each of these right, first time around!
- While pupils will often understand how to draw Keynesian and classical aggregate supply curves, there is an opportunity to increase the challenge by asking them to identify which type of curve is effective in explaining a range of scenarios. For example, you could state that 'the economy is always at its productive capacity in the long run' or that 'increasing aggregate demand can

increase real GDP when there is low consumer confidence' and ask pupils to determine if this relates to a classical or Keynesian model of aggregate supply.

KEY POINTS

- For pupils to be able to retrieve information from their long-term memory, they need to regularly practice remembering what they have been taught without notes.
- This can be done at the start of a lesson as a quiz, for homework or at any point in a lesson.
- Pupils often find retrieval practice harder than re-reading notes and therefore tend not to complete it at home, so it is important they are taught the method's effectiveness.
- In order to stop pupils forgetting information, they need to retrieve prior content at regular intervals.
- To increase the level of challenge from the spacing effect, and how much pupils remember as a result, they need to discriminate between similar topics to understand their subtle differences.

REFERENCES

Agawal, P. (2019) 'Retrieval practice and Blooms taxonomy: do students need fact knowledge before higher order learning?', *Journal of Educational Psychology.* 111, pp. 189-209.

Cepeda, N. J. et al. (2008) 'Spacing Effects in Learning: A Temporal Ridgeline of Optimal Retention', *Psychological Science.* 19 (11), pp. 1095–1102.

Didau, D. and Rose, N. (2016) *What Every Teacher Should Know About Psychology.* Woodbridge: John Catt Educational.

gocognitive (2012) 'Robert Bjork: Using our memory shapes our memory' [online video]. Available at: https://www.youtube.com/watch?v =69VPjsgm-E0. (Accessed 05/02/22).

Horvath, J. (2019) *Stop Talking, Start Influencing: 12 insights from brain to science to make your message stick.* Dunedin: Exisle Publishing.

Kirschner, P. Sweller, J. and Cark, R. (2006) 'Why minimal guidance during instruction does not work: an analysis of the failure of constructivist, discovery, problem-based, experiential and inquiry-based teaching', *Educational Psychologist.* 41.

Murre, J. and Dros, J. (2015) 'Replication and Analysis of Ebbinghaus' Forgetting Curve', *PloS one.* 10.

Roediger, H. L. and Karpicke, J. (2006) 'Test-enhanced learning: taking memory tests improved long-term retention', *Psychological Science.* 17, pp. 249-255.

Roediger, H. L., Putnam, A. L, and Smith, M.A. (2011) 'Ten benefits of testing and their applications to retrieval practice.' In: *Psychology of learning and motivation: Cognition in education.* Mestre, J. and Ross, B. (Eds.) pp. 1-36. Oxford: Elsevier.

Rohrer, D. (2012) 'Interleaving helps students distinguish among similar concepts', *Educational Psychology Review.* 24, pp. 355-367.

Rohrer, D and Taylor, K. (2006) 'The effects of overlearning and distributed practice on the retention of mathematics knowledge', *Applied Cognitive Psychology.* 20, pp. 1209–1224.

Sumeracki, M. Weinstein, Y. and Cavigoli, O. (2018) *Understanding how we learn: A visual Guide.* Abingdon: Routledge.

ASSESSMENT AND FEEDBACK

When I first started teaching, every assessment I would give was a modified version of a past paper. After all, this is what they would do at the end of the course, so it made sense for pupils to be as familiar with this as possible. I had learned about the importance of deliberate practice in teaching and so if I could have pupils sit as many past papers as possible over two years, then surely this would be the best way to ensure my pupils made rapid progress. Right?

Assessment can be one of the most complex areas of teaching to get your head round, and my approach is completely different now to what I've just described. And with good reason. In this chapter, we will look at what the research tells us about constructing assessments, how this can inform how we create assessments in economics and then how these can be used to provide feedback that enables pupils to improve their learning.

WHAT THE RESEARCH SAYS

An old teaching joke (and as with all teaching jokes, not a particularly funny one) goes like this: a teacher says that he has taught a dog to speak German. A disbelieving friend asks him to prove it by asking the dog to speak. 'Oh, he can't speak it,' replies the teacher. 'I have taught him, but he hasn't learned it!' The purpose of assessment is to bridge that divide. To get a handle on how much pupils actually understand of what they have been taught.

Assessment followed by feedback has been shown to be one of the most effective strategies for pupils to make progress (Elliot *et al.*, 2016). Yet feedback is only effective if the assessment itself is reliable, and crafting an assessment that provides information on pupils' gaps in learning is surprisingly complex.

The best definition of assessment to help teachers ensure theirs are fit for purpose is this: assessment is a procedure for drawing inferences (Cronbach, 1971). It is not possible for a pupil to be assessed on every part of their economics curriculum. Even after just a few months on the course, an assessment of everything pupils have been taught would be logistically impossible. Given this, an assessment is designed to enable us as teachers to make inferences about what our pupils know.

It is for this reason that Dylan Wiliam suggests that drawing a distinction between formative and summative assessments (or assessments of and for learning) is not useful. The same assessment can be used summatively or formatively (Wiliam, 2020). Some may be better designed for different purposes, but what teachers should be considering is what inferences can be made from each one.

However, the distinction between a final assessment and an assessment of pupils' understanding remains a useful one when considering how an assessment should be created. Daisy Christodoulou talks about the deliberate practice model, where a model of progression is created, and assessments designed to support it (Christodoulou, 2016). This means that a skill is broken down into its component parts, and each of these is assessed, creating opportunities for pupils to practice these repeatedly with feedback. Only after each component is mastered do pupils put the entire thing together. A common analogy is with sports coaching. A football team will not play a full 11-a-side football match every day but instead will have individual sessions practising dribbling, running, tackling, free kicks, *etc.*

The benefit of this is that feedback is more precise because the task is more specific. And as the task is less complex, working memory should not be overloaded in the process. It might look odd because it means an assessment might look nothing like the final essay or assessment pupils are due to complete, but it is likely to be more effective.

It is common to read about teachers discussing the need for assessments to be valid. However, an assessment itself cannot be valid, only our inferences from the assessments can be valid. This is because an assessment can provide some valid inferences but also poor ones. An assessment with an extract which asks pupils to calculate a good's price elasticity of demand can lead to a valid inference as to the quality of their quantitative skills if they are competent readers. However, if their reading ability is weaker, it is not possible to make this inference as their low marks may be due to an inability to understand the scenario, or an inability to complete the calculation, or both.

The implication for designing a test is that we should not concern ourselves with its validity but rather with what inferences we want to make from it, and whether the assessment lends itself to making those inferences (Wiliam, 2020). In economics, we might start by asking ourselves whether we want to infer pupils' ability to draw diagrams, their understanding of economic theories or their quantitative skills, for example.

In the literature on assessment, this is called construct-irrelevant variance. We can't draw an inference on pupils' quantitative skills with our proposed assessment as their scores are influenced by other areas that we were not trying to assess. Of course, we may want to assess these areas together, but without being able to pinpoint exactly what part of a complex process pupils are getting wrong it becomes difficult to provide them (and ourselves) with useful feedback.

One solution could be to provide a large number of multiple-choice questions. This way, we isolate individual pieces of knowledge, allowing us to draw accurate inferences about what pupils know about certain topics. This would appear to remove construct-irrelevant variance entirely. However, how irrelevant is what is missing? Many would argue that a vital part of economics is to analyse economic essays in depth and apply this to different contexts, so perhaps the 'missing' information is needed after all. This is why it is so important to consider what inferences you want to draw before choosing what type of assessment to give pupils (Thomson, 2019).

Of course, we can draw all of these inferences over time, and so it's worth thinking in terms of a scheme of assessment, much as we do with schemes of work or schemes of learning. What do we want to know about our pupils' learning, at what stage, and how do we build (and interleave) from simple to complex?

Next, and still before constructing our assessment, we need to consider exactly how our assessment will gather the information we will make our inferences from. In the words of Donarski, we must be careful to avoid construct underrepresentation *ie.* our assessment being too small to draw legitimate inferences (Donarski, 2020). This is often referred to as sampling too little of a domain. A one-hour assessment comprising three essays on microeconomics is likely to leave out a large amount of the specification that has been covered, so it will not give us a valid measure of how much pupils know about the course. Too much of the content is untested. That's not to say it doesn't tell us anything, but the question is whether it tells us what we want to know which will help us to push them forward in their learning.

CREATING ECONOMICS ASSESSMENTS

Based on the above information, I will typically only use a past paper for an end-of-year assessment. By this point pupils have had enough practice of each component part of the curriculum, and I have been able to make what I believe are valid inferences about what they do not know in order to provide effective feedback as we have progressed through the course. As part of that journey, they will also have written a number of essays encompassing a range of skills for homework. These, I will discuss in the chapter on that subject (pp. 111-114)..

Throughout the year, my assessments will typically be comprised of multiple-choice question tests, definitions, diagram practice and chains of analysis tables. Let's look at each of these in more detail.

Multiple-choice questions

The most important thing I want to understand in an assessment is if pupils have grasped the core content they need to know. One of the best ways to find that out is using multiple-choice questions. As there is only one correct answer, there can be no discrepancy in the marking to undermine the reliability of the results, which means the validity of my inferences is strong.

Some teachers worry that multiple-choice questionnaires are too simple; pupils can just guess the answers. It's a valid concern, and the easy way to alleviate it is to incorporate a significant number of options and/or astute 'distractor' options. The latter is an option which only appears correct if pupils have fallen foul of a common misconception. By using these, I can make valid inferences about how deeply pupils understand a topic. And if they are choosing the distractor, it is clear where feedback should be targeted. As each question takes little time to answer, it is possible to complete a large number of them, covering a wide range of topics. This reduces concerns about construct underrepresentation, and lends itself extremely well to spaced practice!

There is another concern that may be contributing to this form of assessment's lack of popularity. While multiple-choice is perceived as too simple for pupils, the truth may be more that they are quite complex for teachers. Writing good, challenging multiple-choice questions requires more thought and planning than any other type of question. Fortunately, however, there are a large number of legacy economics papers for A-level and GCSE with well-devised questions. As most of the content remains unchanged and is similar across all exam boards; almost any question from any previous exam can be used. And gathered together in one place, they make an excellent database for quick, reliable and valid assessments.

Definitions

The economics curriculum contains a large number of specialist key terms, and pupils must know and understand their definitions with a high level of familiarity, not least because it is standard in the discipline to define key terms at the start of essays. Therefore, I often give pupils a list of terms to define. The reality is that these will only ever add up to a small sample of what is a vast domain, so I do not look at pupils' marks in any single assessment to make inferences about their understanding of definitions. Instead, I use information across multiple assessments to gradually paint a picture of how much more practice pupils need.

Revisiting simple definitions like this – for example, by asking students to create flashcards initially and then encouraging them to review them – is a simple way to ensure pupils aren't just 're-reading notes' but usefully testing themselves. Simple, factual knowledge like this is precisely the kind where automaticity can be a quick win and, as with multiple choice, excellent fodder for spaced practice.

Diagram practice

Two different inferences can be made from students' diagrams, so to ensure a valid assessment of each component, I design two different assessments.

Initially, I want to know if pupils can remember different diagrams. For this, I will simply give pupils instructions to draw a number of different diagrams. For example: Draw a diagram showing a positive consumption externality. This tells me if pupils can remember how to draw the diagram and label it correctly.

However, this is only a useful initial step. I also want to know if pupils can determine what diagram they should be drawing in a given scenario. So next I give pupils a one-sentence statement and ask them to draw a relevant diagram, without specifying which. This way, I can determine if pupils can use their knowledge of diagrams and apply it in context. For example: Draw a diagram showing the potential market failure caused by education. I am still asking for a positive consumption externality diagram, but this time I have not told them.

Jumping straight to the second type of diagram assessment would reduce the validity of my inferences. If pupils get the answer correct, there is no problem, but if it not it would be impossible to know why. Is my pupil unsure of what type of externality education is? Or did she know, but forget how to draw the diagram? I'd need a second assessment to find out (even if that's just a conversation). But splitting the assessments, not only do I reduce construction-irrelevant variance, but by doing so I also scaffold my assessments, giving my pupils more opportunities for success.

Chains of analysis tables

A key critique of assessments using this deliberate practice model is that they are not relevant for essay-based subjects like economics because they do not assess pupils' ability to fully explain the consequences of a point. This is a misconception based on the assumption that the method treats each piece of information only as a disconnected data point when in fact it simply emphasises the importance of achieving automaticity of recall.

That automaticity is only a first step, and it makes every subsequent step easier.

As a middle step between purely knowledge-based assessments and longer essays, I use chains of analysis tables precisely to assess their ability to connect what they have learned with its real-world consequences. I provide a table that pupils fill in. In the first box is a statement. For example: 'High contestability means there are low barriers to entry.' A further four empty boxes require pupils to enter four links in a chain of consequences from that statement.

This way, it is possible to assess if pupils are able to complete detailed chains of analysis on a topic and provide specific feedback on which links are missing or how chains can be extended. Better yet, they can be used for a multitude of topics. And best of all, when combined these tasks replicate what we want pupils to be able to do by the end of their course: to construct reasoned analysis of economic issues and concepts.

The common way to assess this would be to have pupils write an essay, usually as part of a past paper. Yet imagine pupils scored an average of 48% on an essay about monopolies. It is then difficult to draw valid inferences about what pupils do or do not know. Is it because of a lack of understanding about what monopolies are? Did they understand this but fail to show it on a diagram? Did they know the diagram but not realise it was relevant in a discussion about Apple's market share? Did they understand that but fail to fully explain these points with accurate chains of analysis? Does this mean pupils have similar weaknesses regarding other market structures?

If the assessment does not provide specific inferences, it's impossible to provide effective feedback. But with chains of analysis tables, it is possible to pinpoint exactly where pupils are going wrong and to be highly specific about how to improve. Of course, over time pupils need to be able to put these components together, so this does not negate the need to practice holistic questions or essays. The key thing to remember is that each assessment has its rightful place in the scheme, and what determines that is how well it will enable us to provide timely and meaningful feedback.

I won't dwell here on setting and marking essays. My assumption is that it is a normal and routine part of every economics teacher's practice. Suffice to say that because they are difficult to make valid inferences from – and because they are so time-consuming! – they should only form a specific and limited part of our assessment arsenal. Instead, let's focus on what to do after an assessment. Because even once our assessments are reliable and valid inferences can be drawn from them, they will only be of any use if the feedback they generate effectively enables pupils to make progress. Teachers often refer to the saying that 'weighing the pig does not make it fatter.' In fact, as retrieval practice shows, this is not strictly accurate. Better to say: 'Weighing the pig alone does not make it fatter.'

EFFECTIVE FEEDBACK

The pupil, not the work

The scarcest resource in schools will always be time. Rather than considering what type of feedback will improve pupils the most in absolute terms then, what we really need to ask ourselves is what will enable pupils to make the most improvement relative to the time it takes to prepare the feedback. Individual, personalised comments and actions may provide an additional benefit for pupils, but if it is inefficient in terms of workload – that is, if it is taking teacher time away from some other practice that could present more benefit – then it is not truly an effective form of feedback.

The three biggest challenges with feedback are that it often requires more work from teachers than pupils, that pupils may not understand how to improve, and that it focuses more on the completed tasks than future ones (Hill, 2020). This is why common advice is that feedback should improve the pupil and not the piece of work. But what exactly does this mean?

The assessment approach detailed above, based on CLT and retrieval practice, makes it quite clear. If pupils score poorly on a diagram question, feedback should be on how to improve their diagrams. Modelling and a large amount of practice will soon see their performance improve. This way, they are not perfecting a previous answer (for which the question may never come up again) but improving their ability such that they will be able to apply it in all future pieces of work.

Contrary to what has been expected of teachers for so long (and still is in many places), this does not need to involve individual comments on pupils' work. It is perfectly possible simply to read pupils' answers and provide whole-class feedback to tackle common mistakes. Many teachers have templates for doing this, but the exact pro forma used does not matter. Indeed, I would argue no pro forma is required. What matters is recording the areas that pupils are struggling with, any misconceptions they might have and then, crucially, what pupils can do to improve.

It is possible that this will involve redrafting a piece of work, but it does not have to. What matters most is the knowledge pupils may need to (re) learn. I recently read over some of my pupils' essays evaluating whether a minimum price or indirect tax would be more effective in tackling alcohol over-consumption. Many struggle to compare them because they found many of the disadvantages of each policy were similar. They could not recall the clear differences between the policies and so, instead of redrafting the essay, I re-taught this element and then asked pupils to complete 10 questions to check whether they now understood the difference between them. Armed with the fact that learning is a change in pupils' long-term memory, I asked them to answer similar questions a few weeks later.

A culture of improvement

So much for giving feedback – for it to be effective there is also the knotty question of how it is received. One of the key challenges is to create an environment in which pupils want to improve and use your feedback to do so, rather than simply checking their mark or grade and holding you solely responsible for what happens next. This could lead us into a debate about the effectiveness of providing marks or grades, or the efficacy of delaying feedback, but there is limited evidence to showing how impactful either is. What is more pertinent is to consider how we can ensure pupils take feedback seriously. In his excellent book, *The CRAFT of assessment: A whole-school approach to assessment for learning* (2020), Michael Chiles offers five principles to ensure an effective feedback culture. According to the author, feedback should be:

- timely
- offered within a receptive culture
- granular

- supportive of self-regulation
- a fluid process

The first, third and fifth points are all about how we plan for, structure and give feedback, which we've just covered in depth. As for the second and fourth, an important aspect is the language we use when delivering it. While this still focuses on the teacher rather than the pupil, we have an important role to play in ensuring pupils accept what we say as critique rather than criticism, avoiding defensiveness. To do that, our feedback should be specific and – in a reversal of our maxim above about improving the pupil, not the work – focused on the work, not the individual. For example, if pupils are not accurately labelling a diagram, 'Every axis needs to be labelled' is likely go down better and lead to better progress than 'Your diagrams are too sloppy.'

This might feel like a somewhat nebulous point but evidence shows it is worth getting right, because there is significant variation in the impact of feedback on learning. In a series of meta-studies on the subject, Hattie showed that the effect size of feedback on pupil outcomes varied from -0.04 to 1.24 (Hattie and Timperley, 2007). So, while good feedback can have a substantial positive effect, in theory at least it's possible for bad feedback to make matters worse!

Effective assessment and feedback play a central role in ensuring pupils make good progress. They tell you what pupils know, provide you with the tools to help them improve, and allow you to check going forward that they now know what they did not know previously. However, at the end of this chapter it is worth noting a few caveats.

First, while the focus of this chapter has been on types of formal assessment, assessment can also be informal, and includes anything from a low-stakes quiz to verbal questioning. Anything that provides you with information about what pupils know is assessment. It is important not to fall into the trap of believing that assessing pupils' understanding is something that only happens at the end of term or when a data deadline looms.

Second, much of what is done in terms of feedback is unseen. It is easy to believe that feedback is something stuck into pupils' books or shown in a particular-coloured pen. But often, the most effective feedback is immediate, like a verbal correction as pupils are completing work. In *Teach*

Like Nobody's Watching, Mark Enser posits this question: How would you teach differently if you were left alone to get on with it? (Enser, 2019) I find this especially useful when considering feedback. Ignoring what external observers are expecting to see, the only consideration should be what will help our pupils improve in economics.

KEY POINTS

- Before constructing an assessment, it is important to consider what inferences you are hoping to draw from it.
- In order for inferences to be valid, you need to consider whether the task is assessing precisely what you need to assess to know what your students are capable of and how to push them forward.
- Assessment should be scaffolded, from simpler tasks to support retrieval practice to more complex ones resembling the final assessments students are working towards.
- Assessment tasks should be designed to enable granular feedback.
- Feedback is about improving pupils' overall abilities, not their performance on a specific task.
- On the other hand, feedback should always be focused on the work, not the pupil, in order to create a culture of critique, not criticism.

REFERENCES

Chiles, M. (2020) *The CRAFT Of Assessment: A whole school approach to assessment for learning*. Woodbridge: John Catt Educational.

Christodoulou, D. (2016) *Making good progress? The future of assessment for learning*. Oxford: Oxford University Press.

Cronbach, L. J. (1971) 'Test Validation.' In: Thorndike, R. L. (ed.) *Educational Measurement*. pp. 443-507.

Donarski, S. (2020) *The researchED guide to assessment*. Woodbridge: John Catt Educational.

Elliott, V., Baird, J., Hopfenbeck, T. N., Ingram, J., Thompson, I., Usher, N., Zantout, M., Richardson, J. and Coleman, R. (2016) *A Marked Improvement? A Review of the Evidence on Written Marking*. Oxford: Education Endowment Foundation.

Enser, M. (2019). *Teach like nobody's watching: The essential guide to effective and efficient teaching.* Carmarthern: Crown House Publishing.

Hattie, J. and Timperley, H. (2007) 'The Power of Feedback', *Review of Educational Research.* 77(1), pp. 81–112.

Hill, C. (2020) 'Assessment and feedback: An efficiency model for English'. In: Donarski, S. (Ed.) and Bennett, T. (Series Ed.) *The researchED guide to assessment.* Woodbridge: John Catt Educational.

Thomson, D. (2019) *How reliable are KS2 tests?* [online] Available at: https://ffteducationdatalab.org.uk/2019/04/how-reliable-are-key-stage-2-tests/ (Accessed 05/02/2022).

Wiliam, D. (2020) 'How to think about assessment'. In: Donarski, S. (Ed.) and Bennett, T. (Series Ed.) *The researchED guide to assessment.* Woodbridge: John Catt Educational.

↑ CHALLENGE

One of the most complicated aspects of teaching is how to ensure there is a high level of challenge in lessons so that pupils are constantly thinking hard. Often, this is interpreted to mean teachers should design specific activities to stretch those with high prior attainment. It's linked in our professional discourse with the notion of differentiation – or planning work at different levels so that all pupils can access learning. In recent years, teachers are more often given to talking about 'teaching to the top', in the sense of putting appropriate scaffolding in place so that all pupils can access higher-order work. While the latter is preferable, it still suffers from the same problem: genericism. What is often missing is a clear explanation of exactly what deep thinking and challenge look like in the classroom, and that's because the answer is phase- and subject-specific. This chapter is therefore dedicated to six different ways to make economics lessons (accessibly) challenging.

The first thing to note is that challenge is *not* specifically about high prior attainers. Achieving a change in our long-term memory is a challenge, not matter what our starting point is. That's because, for information to ever reach our long-term memory, we need to think deeply about it.

In our earlier chapter, we talked about the distinction between retrieval storage – the information that has made it into pupils' long-term memory – and retrieval strength – the ease with which they can get that information back out. We also referred to Daniel Willingham's famous definition of memory as 'the residue of thought' (Willingham, 2010). We remember what we think about. Challenge is therefore any classroom activity that requires all pupils to think hard about a subject in order either to increase the amount they know or to improve their ability to recall and use that information.

What challenge is not is pupils trying to work out a topic for themselves, as proponents of discovery learning might argue. By and large our pupils are novices, and cognitive science is clear that explicit instruction is the most effective way to teach a novice learner. So having said that, here are six practical ways that challenge can be incorporated into every economics lesson.

DESIRABLE DIFFICULTIES

Robert and Elizabeth Bjork have written extensively on the subject of desirable difficulty (Bjork and Bjork, 1994), a level of challenge that is enough so that pupils will have to think hard and remember content but not so high that they are unable to access work. There are a number of very practical ways desirable difficulties can be introduced into economics lessons, and two techniques that I find particularly helpful when considering challenge specifically.

Mix it up

The first is to vary practice, or to ensure that practice is not always done in the same format. While so much of what we are taught about teaching rightly relates to consistency and routines, there is evidence that varying practice can be beneficial for pupil learning. Let's take calculation questions when teaching elasticities as our example.

When I first started teaching, I would often provide a table where pupils had to calculate the price elasticity of demand (PED) for a variety of examples. It involved lots of practice. Check. And students developed fluency and automaticity. Check. But they only ever manipulated the information in one way. When faced with the same problem in a different context, they floundered. Now I vary this practice. Initially, I give pupils the percentage change in demand and price, and ask them to calculate the PED. The next time, I might give them a small extract from which they need to identify the data related to price and demand, calculate the percentage change themselves, and then the PED. For another task, I might provide the PED and the change in price, and ask pupils to calculate the change in demand. Because the practice is constantly changing, pupils are always having to think deeply about it.

Positive discrimination

The second way to introduce desirable difficulties in the classroom relates back to our chapter on retrieval practice. You'll remember Bjork from that chapter saying that 'using your memory, shapes your memory'. You'll also remember the importance of 'discriminating between ideas', which stems from the same author. But while evidence tells us that comparing and contrasting different ideas is far superior to the mass practice of single topics, actually deploying that in the classroom can result in carnage. When I first read Bjork, I tried to teach a lesson on elasticity, followed by one on market structures and then another on cost-push inflation. The result, predictably, was confusion and anarchy. I had fundamentally misunderstood what Bjork was getting at!

We economics teachers are lucky. The subject is full of interlinked concepts and topics, so there are endless opportunities for discrimination. However, in order for pupils to do this effectively, they must still be taught and practice each topic individually first. It is only over time that practice can achieve the complexity – the challenge – of discriminating between topics.

Once they have the requisite prior learning, my favourite way to challenge them to go beyond it is to explore differences and similarities. For example, when teaching monopolistic competition, I ask pupils in what ways it is similar to and different from a monopoly, and how it resembles or differs from perfect competition. By this point, pupils have learned all three and practised with definitions, multiple-choice questions and chains of analysis tables. These compare and contrast questions now encourage pupils to carefully consider the nuanced differences between each concept. Similarly, when teaching inflation, I ask pupils the difference between cost-push and demand-pull inflation. I give them a number of examples and ask them to explain whether each one is an example of cost-push or demand-pull inflation. I also ask them to set out the similarities and differences between inflation and disinflation.

But at no point does this become an effort in discovery learning. I have taught all of the content explicitly and pupils have practised each component part initially. Only then can they be expected to compare them in a way that allows them to truly think deeply about each concept and the connections between them.

And nor am I engaging in the time-consuming practice of task differentiation. I typically use booklets for this, and before each set of questions I provide some notes about each topic as a scaffold for those who require it. But all pupils are still answering the same question, and the support is there for everyone who needs it. There is of course a risk that all pupils will choose to make use of the scaffolding for ease. This requires the same culture of discipline in the classroom as we discussed briefly earlier in respect of homework. There needs to be a clear expectation that the support material is only there if needed – and should preferably not be needed. In my experience though, the time it takes to read the notes before completing the task means most pupils will not do this unless they really need to.

KNOWLEDGE OF THE HINTERLAND

We will return to these concepts in more detail in our chapter on curriculum, but core and hinterland knowledge are important to our consideration of challenge in the economics classroom, so let's nail them down now. Core knowledge is the fundamental information contained within the specification, that all pupils must understand. In contrast, Christine Counsell, who introduced the concept of hinterland knowledge, defines it as 'vital property that makes curriculum work as a narrative' (Counsell, 2018).

If our teaching is reduced to the core knowledge alone, then not only is the opportunity for wider challenge (and therefore potentially the highest marks) missed, but the magic of the subject is lost. But hinterland knowledge isn't about adding in activities or irrelevant tangents we believe pupils will find 'fun'. Rather, it is those extra stories and historical contexts that give meaning to what is being taught. It helps pupils understand the links between different topics, to stop seeing them as a random collection of facts and graphs and start to weave these into a narrative.

In economics, this is especially important if we want pupils to think deeply about how the subject relates to the pressing issues of the day. When teaching specialisation and the division of labour, I talk about colonialism and the notion that countries can grow wealthier through trade and cooperation instead of imperialism. Similarly, when teaching Marx, I explicitly place his economic theories in the context of Victorian-era working conditions and how governments responded by reforming capitalism, by banning child labour, for example, and creating a system of free education.

I will sometimes be asked: 'But Mr Hamid, will this be in the exam?' And the fact is that hinterland knowledge is not necessarily core knowledge pupils will be assessed on. But it gives real meaning to what is being taught, and that will undoubtedly help them to write better answers, let alone be better economists. Social and historical context helps to bring together different topics too. Specialisation and the division of labour, but also inequality, labour markets and the price mechanism all interlink in a discussion on colonialism.

This year, we discussed the development of the Covid-19 vaccine. We took in the role of the price mechanism, profit incentives, and contrasted the Prime Minister's comments on the innovative power of capitalism with other behavioural economic considerations, including altruism as a motive.

Every year, when discussing the limitations of GDP as a measure of national health in macroeconomics, I take the time to introduce Simon Kuznets, who helped the U.S. Department of Commerce to standardise the measurement of GNP in 1934. We consider why, when he was asked to devise a measure of output, he specifically asked that it not become a target or be used as a general measure of a nation's welfare. I show them Robert F. Kennedy's famous 1968 University of Kansas speech about what GDP does not cover, and I introduce some of the writings of feminist economists about the lack of unpaid labour in these figures.

All of this hinterland knowledge makes the conventional critique of GDP easier to remember and makes economics more than a syllabus. The clear narrative is what makes it a true curriculum. In the end, it's also much more stretching and more challenging – and altogether more rewarding – for pupils than the addition of a 'challenge question'. It ensures all pupils are thinking deeply about the content they are learning and how it relates both to issues of the day and to other topics they have previously learned.

LOOKING TO THE HORIZON

In *Teach to the Top*, Megan Mansworth recommends teachers think about what an undergraduate student would know about a topic as a way of considering what content to include as part of the planning process (Mansworth, 2021). The idea is not to turn an economics A-level into a degree-level course, but to consider where more detailed knowledge can be dipped into while teaching.

For me, this isn't necessarily about adding content. Realistically, with a lot of content to teach over two years, there is limited scope to add in very much at all, and I certainly won't have to explain the problem of scarce time and unlimited content to economics teachers! Instead, Mansworth's book has led me to give close consideration to the type of reading material I expose my students to.

Recently, I taught my Year 12 class about government intervention to correct market failure. Following discussions about minimum prices and Scotland's introduction of a minimum price for alcohol, we read an academic journal article assessing the policy's impact on alcohol consumption compared with nations who have opted to impose taxes instead. I certainly needed to support my pupils to access some of the quantitative analysis, but with that scaffolding in place the reading led to a high level of challenge (and some more hinterland knowledge). Not only did they have a chance to assess the real-world impact of economic policies, but also to experience – most of them for the first time – the work of academic economists.

While academic texts need to be carefully selected to ensure they are accessible, websites like VoxEU.org do an excellent job in making such writing student-friendly while maintaining a high level of rigour. Resources like this are invaluable, because they provide pupils with a wealth of real-world examples with which to enrich their understanding of and ability to apply economic knowledge. Over time, as they gain in confidence to read these journals, they can start to do so independently. Which won't just help their university lecturers, but enrich your experience of teaching them too!

As well as economic journals, pupils can now access LSE lectures online for free too, as well as reports from economic think-tanks and relevant TED talks from economists. It is important to be wary of the political bias in some of these sources, so I always remind pupils that there are different perspectives, and that sources are not necessarily impartial. Critically evaluating the content and credibility of sources can also be modelled in class, of course, which not only helps them to develop as economists, but as citizens.

As with all challenge activities, it is important to remember that accessing such resources is not extension material for some but a way of manageably increasing the difficulty level for all.

KEEPING PARTICIPATION HIGH

Too often, challenge is reduced to an extra question for a pupil who has already completed earlier work. In *Teach like a champion*, Doug Lemov refers to the level of student participation in deep thinking as the 'participation ratio', and challenges us to think about how we keep that ratio consistently as high as possible.

The simplest way to ensure the class participation ratio is high is independent practice, where all pupils are silently completing work in writing. This makes it possible to quickly observe who is working and who isn't. As long as the activity is challenging enough then it is quickly clear that all pupils are thinking hard, and so are being challenged.

But there are a number of different ways that we can ensure that all pupils are participating in deep thinking during a lesson. As I've already mentioned multiple times, economics has the distinct advantage that so many of its key concepts and ideas are interlinked. We really are very lucky in that regard, because among other advantages we've already covered, it is very easy to continuously question pupils verbally on prior content. For example, a lesson on market failure is an excellent opportunity to ask about the price mechanism and efficient allocation of resources.

But questioning alone doesn't guarantee a high participation ratio. If only one pupil is answering a question at a time, it's not clear the other 29 in the class have gained anything from that interaction. But by combining two strategies from Lemov's book, we can transform our questioning into an activity that encourages all pupils to think hard.

First, and most famously, is an activity called cold calling, which simply entails asking questions of specific pupils of your choosing as opposed to those with their hands up. At a basic level, it ensures all pupils are doing some thinking about the answer as any of them might be chosen to give it. But it's no guarantee they will all be thinking hard about it.

For example, I could ask 'Lily, what were the three functions of our price mechanism again?' but the moment I have chosen Lily, all the other pupils can relax. I can improve this by keeping the pupil's name until the end of the question, asking instead 'What are the three functions of the price mechanism, Lily?' This still isn't ideal, because just as the class are starting to think of an answer, Lily's name acts as a get-out-of-jail-free card.

This is where our second *Teach like a champion* technique comes into its own: wait time. This is a subtle but important difference whereby there is a pause between asking the question and choosing who will answer it. Now, I am asking 'What are the functions of the price mechanism … Lily?' so that all pupils need to be thinking about the answer before they find out who needs to answer it. Asking a verbal question in this way leads to the entire class experiencing the full level of challenge that questioning can offer. However, the cold calling/wait time combo's success depends on classroom culture too. Students must know that they can get answers wrong, but equally that having to repeat a question because they weren't listening is unacceptable. In essence, reaching the highest participation ratio requires there to be a minimum participation level below which none should fall.

Another potential pitfall for verbal questioning is that it lends itself well to short-answer questions, but many of the questions we want to ask are more complex. If I ask, 'Why would a classical economist believe that the free market will always lead to an efficient allocation of resources … Lily?' her answer is likely to take three to four minutes – long enough for others to switch off. Some conclude that for this reason cold call is less effective at A-level.

Fortunately, there are relatively simple ways of ensuring that pupils are still listening to the answer and thinking about what has been said. Science teacher Adam Boxer has set out a number of these which I have found useful:

- What did he/she say? Asking pupils to repeat what has just been said is a simple way to check that they are still listening. After a few times (with relevant sanctions if appropriate), all pupils will understand that they need to listen not just to the question but to their peers' answers too.

- What was the question? It's too easy for pupils to say they don't know an answer to a question to avoid trying to answer it. Ask them what the question was, and if they can't answer that, then accept no excuse. Over time, challenging pupils in this way will build a culture where everyone knows they are expected to listen all the time.

- How could you improve that? Asking pupils what their classmates got wrong or could have said more means everyone has to listen intently and think hard about their answer.

(Boxer, 2020)

WHAT A GREAT ONE LOOKS LIKE

There are various reasons for using an exemplar or model answer after pupils have completed an essay. Sometimes, this is so that pupils can understand how a question should be answered. At A-level, this is often a way to ensure they can satisfy the assessment objectives of a particular exam board. Usually, it is pitched at a level pupils can attain in the allotted time so that they have something to aim for.

While there is nothing wrong with providing additional scaffolding or deconstructing a standard model answer to show how assessment objectives can be met – and, indeed, clear modelling is necessary when first introducing pupils to essay-writing – it can be a missed opportunity to introduce additional challenge into lessons. Sometimes, I just write an answer to a question, without any consideration for exam criteria or structures. I do this to show my pupils how creative answers to a question can be produced, bringing in a variety of different topics to write a synoptic answer.

As well as writing my own, I often show articles in academic journals answering similar questions so that pupils can experience challenging texts and see what work can potentially be produced in the subject. These are often available for free online, and many schools have JSTOR access so that more can be accessed. If these are too complex, then teaching publications like *Economics Today* and *Economics Review* can be a nice halfway house.

There is an important caveat, however. While this is useful to promote academic rigour, it runs the risk of confusing pupils. Warn them that this is an opportunity to challenge themselves and to see what can be done, rather than something for them to copy (especially if they are not yet ready).

DON'T APOLOGISE FOR THE SUBJECT

For each of us, there are parts of economics that we simply don't enjoy as much as others. For me, I never look forward with great excitement to teaching different types of economies and diseconomies of scale. When I first started teaching, I would often say things like, 'I know this isn't the most interesting of topics, but we need to get through it.' I shudder when I think of this now. The message that went out to pupils was loud and clear: this isn't worth paying attention to.

Part of challenge is ensuring that pupils are constantly motivated to listen and engage in what is being taught. In *The Learning Rainforest* (2017), Tom Sherrington talks about inspiring joy in your subject. For me, part of this is ensuring we never apologise for it. We are in the very fortunate position of teaching the greatest subject in the world and pupils need to understand what a pleasure it is to be in your classroom.

Everything is difficult, but everything is worth learning.

KEY POINTS

- Challenge is not about 'stretching high attainers' but for all pupils.
- If pupils are not thinking deeply about content, they will not remember it.
- Try to vary what pupils practice to create 'desirable difficulties'.
- Consider opportunities for pupils to discriminate between different topics.

- Additional hinterland knowledge can enrich the subject beyond the limits of the syllabus.
- Don't be scared of introducing high academic rigour into lessons, even if these are beyond the key stage being taught.
- Keep the participation ratio high so that all pupils are thinking about what they are learning.
- Never apologise for what you are teaching!

REFERENCES

Bjork, E. L., & Bjork, R. A. (2011) 'Making things hard on yourself, but in a good way: Creating desirable difficulties to enhance learning'. In: Gernsbacher, M. A., Pew, R. W., Hough, L. M. and Pomerantz, J. R. (Eds.) & FABBS Foundation, *Psychology and the real world: Essays illustrating fundamental contributions to society*, pp. 56–64. New York: Worth Publishers.

Boxer, A. (2020) *Ratio*. [online] Available at   https://achemicalorthodoxy. wordpress.com/2020/02/09/ratio/ (Accessed 05/02/22).

Counsell, C. (2018) *Senior curriculum leadership 1: The indirect manifestation of knowledge: (A) curriculum as narrative.* [online] Available at: https:// thedignityofthethingblog.wordpress.com/2018/04/07/senior-curriculum- leadership-1-the-indirect-manifestation-of-knowledge-a-curriculum-as- narrative/ (Accessed 05/02/2022).

Mansworth, M. (2021) *Teach to the Top: Aiming high for every learner.* Woodbridge: John Catt Educational.

Sherrington, T. (2017) *The Learning Rainforest: Great teaching in real classrooms.* Woodbridge: John Catt Educational.

Willingham, D. (2010) *Why Don't Students Like School? A cognitive scientist answers questions about how the mind works and what it means for the classroom.* San Francisco: Jossey Bass.

EXPLICIT INSTRUCTION

THE IMPORTANCE OF DIRECT INSTRUCTION

I can still vividly remember my first ever economics lesson. I faced a group of enthusiastic year 12 pupils, ready for their first experience of A-level economics and I was going to guide them in their discovery of scarcity and the economic problem. If they didn't know what these concepts meant or how they linked together, then they were in trouble from the start because I certainly had no intention of explaining it to them.

First, I asked my new pupils to look at a case study about a coffee shop in Angel tube station (note the use of a local area to them to make this lesson super-cool and relevant). I wasn't going to waste time and stifle their creativity by telling them why we were talking about coffee shops. Instead, I chose to pose some questions.

'Why is the coffee more expensive than in nearby outlets?' I asked, expecting nothing short of an epiphany about supply and demand. Many people want the coffee but there is only one supplier in the station, which makes the coffee valuable, would come the answer. I would congratulate them on the fact that, even though they did not know it, they had fallen onto the meaning of scarcity and the economic principle that a mismatch of resources and needs creates value.

From there, I would ask them who makes the most profit from the venture, and through the power of think-pair-share alone they would soon realise that the scarce resource is not really the coffee but the location of the business, so it is the landlord who receives the greatest return given the high rents charged on this prime piece of real estate.

Their jaws would drop to the floor in amazement at how they had learned these pearls of economic wisdom without even realising it. They might not, but they would certainly be justified if they now chose to stand on the desk proclaiming 'O Captain! My Captain!' while the headteacher waited outside with a 'teacher of the year' award.

For some inexplicable reason, none of this came to pass. Instead, unsurprisingly, pupils had no idea why the coffee was more expensive. After some discussion, a few of them guessed what I was thinking and stumbled on the right answer. Most did not.

Unperturbed, I proceeded to the next part of my meticulously planned discovery lesson to show how scarcity leads to choices that lead to the economic problem. Not that I wasted valuable discovery time explaining any of that. Instead, I gave them a new worksheet where they could find it all out for themselves.

They would now work in groups and decide how much money each stakeholder receives. During this discussion, it would suddenly dawn on them that it was not possible to satisfy everyone's demands and – Eureka! – that scarcity means choices must be made. By their own powers of deduction, they would have just discovered the economic problem.

Except that they didn't. They spent the time discussing their favourite coffee instead.

The problem is that I was teaching novice learners, and they had no bank of knowledge (or information in their long-term memories) to draw upon to make these 'discoveries'. Newton spoke about standing on the shoulders of giants, but my pupils had their feet firmly on the floor and, for all intents and purposes, I had no intention of giving them a leg up.

With no long-term memory to draw upon, all we have is our working memory with which to process new information. And we've already learned that working memory has a very limited capacity. So, the inevitable intrinsic load was already high, but the way I presented information in my 'lesson' added a huge amount of extraneous load. I actually impeded my pupils' learning.

Rather than devoting their limited working memory to thinking about scarcity, they were thinking about how a coffee shop works, which coffee is more expensive, thinking about what the differences are, what the coffee in Angel station is like, if an employee deserves more money than a manager, *etc.* Effectively, anything and everything apart from what I wanted them to think about: what scarcity is and how it leads to the economic problem.

As Clark, Kirschner, and Sweller have explained, when teaching a novice learner, we can reduce extraneous load and optimise their thinking about the actual content by explicitly teaching what we want pupils to understand so that they devote their processing ability to that and only that (Clark, Kirschner and Sweller, 2006).

Unsurprisingly, those pupils who already knew a bit about scarcity just about understood what I was saying. The rest left my lesson as clueless as they'd entered it. If the purpose of teaching is to effect a change in long-term memory, I had abjectly failed.

WHAT THE RESEARCH SAYS

While the importance of direct or explicit instruction for teaching novice learners has been about a regular topic of teacher conversation in recent years, how to actually explain things is often neglected. Siegfried Engelmann pioneered a method of scripted instruction called Direct Instruction (the capitalisation marks it out from more generic approaches) which provides a useful framework for how using examples can ensure pupils clearly understand what is being taught.

In itself, the notion of using an example to explain a point is so obvious it's barely worth mentioning in a book about how to teach. Yet the choice of how many and which examples to use is quite complex. There are two important propositions we need to consider when determining how to teach via examples. The first is that pupils have the capacity to learn any feature 'that is exemplified through examples' (Engelmann and Carnine, 1982). So, if we were to teach pupils about a dog with common features like height, size *etc* then by showing numerous different examples of dogs with different features means pupils will be able to understand what a dog is (Needham, 2020). It means the onus is on teachers to ensure the correct examples have been used as pupils should be able to understand any concept with common characteristics.

The second proposition is that pupils have the 'capacity to generalize to new examples on the basis of sameness of quality' (Engelmann and Carnine, 1982). As pupils hear different examples of a dog then they will automatically note in their minds what the commonalities are in the examples to develop mental rules. This is inductive reasoning as pupils will use the similarities in examples for a generalised understanding of what is being taught.

In his chapter in the excellent *researchED guide to explicit and direct instruction*, Tom Needham distilled these two propositions into four logical facts about presenting examples (Needham, 2020):

1. It is logically impossible to teach a concept through the presentation of one example.
2. It is logically impossible to present a group of positive examples that communicates only one interpretation.
3. Any sameness shared by both positive and negative examples rules out a possible interpretation.
4. A negative example rules out the maximum number of interpretations when the negative example is least different from some positive example.

Engelmann spoke of three clear principles to consider when selecting examples and non-examples (examples where the concept being explained does not occur) (Engelmann, 1982).

First is the difference principle. When choosing an example and non-example, Engelmann says, they should be highly similar so that the only difference pupils are drawn to is the specific difference we want them to understand. Ideally done with more than two examples, with examples all sharing many of the same features, the minimal difference demonstrates the limit of the concept we are teaching.

Second is the sameness principle, which states that when looking at positive examples, they should be as different to each other as possible. In contrast to the difference principle, what we want to draw pupils' attention to here is what makes the positive examples the same. And to do that effectively, we need our examples to be maximally different so that they only see the few similarities that explain the key characteristics of the concept. When explaining what a dog is, for example. it makes sense to choose a chihuahua, a poodle and an Irish wolfhound to demonstrate that dogs come in strikingly different shapes (Watkins and Slocum, 2003).

And third is the setup principle. As Engelmann put it, we should choose examples and non-examples that 'share the greatest possible number of irrelevant features'. This is similar to the difference principle, but the focus here is on inferring the characteristics that are relevant to defining our concept and which are not, rather than inferring the definition itself. 'Setting up' examples with plenty of irrelevant features supports students to quickly see past distractions and work their way through complex problems more efficiently.

Beyond Engelmann, an additional aspect of teaching through examples that is rarely discussed (and often problematic) is the use of an initial concrete example as part of direct instruction. Our tendency – perhaps because it is the example that was set for us by our teachers at school and our teacher training mentors – is to explain a concept and to quickly follow that up with: 'For example...' The problem is that pupils are already processing an abstract concept they haven't understood properly yet, and we are immediately asking them to connect it with a concrete example. The load on their working memories is simply too high to guarantee they will all make the leap.

Science teacher Pritesh Raichura speaks of reversing this trend and instead going from concrete to abstract (Raichura, 2019). By starting with examples that everyone will be able to understand and relate to, like sweating after exercise or shivering when it's cold, we can gradually build towards explaining what homeostasis is. This should not increase the time taken to explain a concept – though it might, which would only demonstrate that our prior pace was probably too fast – but the reversal of the instruction sequence is far more likely to ensure all students retain the information.

To sum up, we want to start with a concrete example followed by multiple examples that are very different so that pupils focus on the few similarities. After this, we can introduce a non-example (or false example) where the concept does not hold. This should be as similar as possible to some of the previous examples, both in content and with the same superficial information so that pupils will only focus on what makes the examples different.

Simple enough, but what does that look like in the economics classroom? It would certainly be remiss for a chapter about using examples not to offer any. So, let's look at some concrete ways we can apply Direct Instruction to support our curriculum.

DIRECT INSTRUCTION IN ECONOMICS

Diminishing marginal utility

Before getting into any abstract explanations of what diminishing marginal utility is, I start with a concrete example in the form of an anecdote: I opened a packet of Munchies this morning and really, really enjoyed the first one. I hadn't had Munchies in ages and I happened to be craving sugar. By the second one, the novelty had worn off. By the fifth, my sugar craving was satisfied. Halfway through the packet, I was still enjoying them, but a lot less. I went on to finish the packet, but I started regretting it long before I'd eaten the last one!

Nobody who's ever binged on their favourite sweet (and isn't that everyone?) is going to struggle to understand this example. From there, I go on to explain that a consumer could seek an accountancy service, a shipping container, or a pet dog. They'll initially get a certain level of satisfaction, but are likely to get less extra satisfaction from each extra dog they get. The idea of these examples is to make them so different to the first that students make use of the sameness principle and understand that the type of good being consumed doesn't matter; Diminishing marginal utility still applies. Only at this point do I introduce the term itself and provide a technical definition.

But something is still missing: a non-example. So, I round off by explaining why having a packet of Munchies and then getting less satisfaction from eating a Mars bar is not diminishing marginal utility, because they are different goods. The use of another confectionary is deliberate. The similarity of the goods makes clear use of the difference principle.

Inflation

When introducing concepts that some pupils already have some understanding of from watching the news – like inflation – I find I often need to be extra careful in my selection of examples. This is because, in order to make the boundaries of the concept clear, I also need to unpack any potential misconceptions pupils are bringing into the classroom.

However, the principles remain the same. I begin by discussing how, when I was younger, my uncle would give me £1 and I would go to the local corner shop and buy a number of sweets. Today that same pound would only buy one thing. Everything is so much more expensive! After letting them consider for a moment quite how many sweets my pound used to get me, I then introduce the concept of inflation as a sustained rise in the general price level.

I then show them some data showing the change in prices over time and crucially make these for very different types of goods to make full use of the sameness principle. So, my charts show a change in the price of Freddos and also the change in the price of lawyers' hourly rates. This helps pupils understand that we are talking about a rise in the general price level and not of one particular good or set of goods. I also ensure that each example shows price changes over a prolonged time period to emphasise that this is a sustained increase in the price level, not a temporary spike.

The common misconception when teaching inflation is that it is a rise in the price of one particular good rather than the general price level of all goods, so this is what I focus my non-examples on. I then discuss the spike in the price of hand sanitiser during the first Covid lockdown due to unprecedented demand to explain why this is not inflation because it only applies to one good (or perhaps a set of goods, if we take PPE prices more generally), but not in the general price level. Similarly, I show them examples of intra-day commodity price volatility to demonstrate that rises don't represent inflation because they are not sustained.

Deflation and disinflation

Linked to inflation are the concepts of deflation and disinflation, which continue to befuddle everyone from economics pupils to politicians and economic correspondents who really should know better! Here, a good concrete example can eliminate any potential misconceptions at source.

I tell the story of my nephew getting taller. Initially, he was growing at a rapid rate (in percentage terms), but now he has started to grow at a slower rate. Nevertheless, while he is not growing as fast, he is still growing and certainly hasn't shrunk. That final part usually elicits a few groans because it's so blindingly obvious that it seems not worth even mentioning. And yet it's a crucial detail before the abstraction involved in defining disinflation as a reduction in the rate of inflation. Prices are still increasing! Only then do I go further by showing my pupils data and helping them to determine whether it shows deflation or disinflation.

While the terms are initially confusing, once students have practised with a decent number of examples there is a benefit in their apparent similarity: deflation and disinflation work as non-examples of each other! A reduction in prices is not the same as a reduction in the rate of inflation, and vice versa. Further practice in categorising a wide variety of numerical examples as inflation, deflation or disinflation tends to be very effective at ensuring the economic correspondents of the future will indeed know better. Or, at least, that more of their audience will know when they are being misinformed.

Private and external costs

When I first started teaching economics, one key concept I was always surprised to find pupils struggled with a lot was the difference between private and external costs. Perhaps guilty of that psychological bias I referred to earlier as the 'curse of knowledge', I couldn't really understand where the confusion was, so I would skirt past the issue relatively quickly. This is an area where examples and non-examples have proved transformative for my pupils' understanding.

I start with the example of someone buying and smoking a packet of cigarettes, which damages their health (I guess it could be a packet of Munchies, but there are some of my own biases I'd rather not challenge!). Then I use an example of someone over-using a sunbed, someone buying a Ferrari, and someone buying a facemask. The wide variety of examples help to show the different types of private costs, from financial to health and from the smallest to the largest good.

I then return to my smoking example to discuss the impact of ill health on the NHS and thereby all taxpayers, including non-smokers. I compare the different costs to the smoker and the NHS before defining the more abstract concepts of external and social costs. I then ask pupils to differentiate between the example and non-example by asking them to explain why a consumer becoming ill due to smoking is a private and not an external cost. The key is to use the same example for external cost, making use of the sameness principle in a slightly different context.

I then return to my earlier examples and discuss the environmental external costs of the Ferrari and the sunbed use to show the difference between the private and external costs associated with of all of these. I finish this section by jumbling up the examples and asking pupils to determine whether each scenario I mention represents a private or external cost and to justify their decisions. The facemask example is a useful link to the next section of learning, when we will discuss private and external benefits.

The important point about this process is that, while initially it seems to take a lot longer than simply explaining a concept's definition, it actually leads to considerably improved efficiency. A greater understanding of these terms first time around means there is much less re-explaining and feedback required later. In my experience, the more I have focused on clear teacher explanations using examples, the quicker I have been able to move through content.

Price takers

Market structures have a reputation as a difficult and (unjustly, in my view) dry topic to learn. I find this is particularly true when teaching perfect competition and the notion of being a price taker. However, the use of a good concrete example – and this one is my absolute favourite – has been transformative for me and my pupils here too. I start off by recounting an episode of *The Fresh Prince of Bel Air* in which geeky Carlton wears his jacket inside out after seeing his impossibly cool cousin, Will, do the same. Carlton wants to be an influencer among his friends, but his total lack of social clout means nobody follows him.

'But what's this got to do with economics, Mr Hamid?' Well, a firm can't influence the market price of a good by varying output when they lack market share. This means they must charge the same market price as their competitors. My non-example to explain the boundary of this concept is of firms who are forced to charge the same price due to regulation. I then go into more depth with more positive examples demonstrating the consequences of charging above or below market price.

Typically, I don't introduce more non-examples in detail until we are looking at alternative market structures. At that point, they can be constantly compared to show the boundary of each concept, and I usually do so through a test in which pupils categorise statements into different market structures to ensure they fully understand the different characteristics of each.

This process of going from concrete to abstract and using multiple examples to highlight their commonalities and differences and then using non-examples to show concept boundaries can be used to explain almost everything in economics, and it has revolutionised my teaching.

In fact, I often reflect on the fact that there must be many, many more examples and non-examples than I could ever come up with on my own. If there is any contribution the growing community of economics teachers on social media could make to our common disciplinary knowledge, it is surely this. Such a shared resource, cataloguing a list of concept-specific different examples for each of us to use (and occasionally freeload from each other!) would doubtless enrich all of our teaching experiences and save us all time in the classroom. Because if there is one downside we can't get away from, it is the fact that coming up with them initially does add to workload.

KEY POINTS

- Use multiple and varied examples to explain a concept.
- Use examples that are as different as possible so that pupils make the correct inferences about their commonalities.
- Use non-examples to show the boundaries beyond which a concept does not hold.
- Ensure non-examples are as similar as possible to the positive examples to enable pupils to draw the correct inferences about their differences.

- Examine an initial, concrete example before explaining the topic in an abstract way so that pupils have something relatable to connect the more abstract concept to.

REFERENCES

Engelmann, S. (1992) *War against the schools' academic child abuse*. Portland, OR: Halcyon House.

Engelmann, S. and Carnine, D. (1982). *Theory of Instruction: Principles and applications*. New York: Irvington Publishing, Inc.

Needham, T. (2020) 'Teaching through examples'. In: Boxer, A. (Ed.) and Bennett, T. (Series Ed.)*The researchED guide to explicit and direct instruction*. Woodbridge: John Catt Educational.

Raichura, P (2019) *Clear teacher explanations 1: Examples and non-examples*. [online] Available at: https://bunsenblue.wordpress.com/2019/10/20/clear-teacher-explanations-i-examples-non-examples/ (Accessed 05/02/2022).

Watkins, C, & Slocum, T. A. (2003). 'Elements of Direct Instruction', *Journal of Direct Instruction*. 3, pp. 4-32.

↑ IMPROVING PUPILS' WRITING

'I know it, I just can't explain it!' is an answer we are all too familiar with. Fortunately, there are a variety of techniques we can employ which will help our pupils to develop their written and verbal fluency in economics. These are arguably the most important skills pupils have to develop: the use of a wide variety of economics terms to construct meaningful points about the impacts of various factors on an equally varied number of stakeholders, using developed chains of reasoning.

As pupils get closer to assessments, their need to be able to articulate their points of view becomes critical to their success in the subject – a key area of assessment. This chapter looks at this signature aspect of the pedagogy of economics: the practical techniques that we can employ right from the first lesson to ensure that our pupils remember what we teach them to enable them to articulate their points of view eloquently, both verbally and in written answers. Economics also requires pupils to use data appropriately to explain their analyses, so this chapter also includes techniques to improve pupils' numeracy skills.

By the end of this chapter, you should be able to create resources that will ensure your pupils can develop written and verbal chains of reasoning, and to embed numeracy into all your economics lessons.

BUILDING A KNOWLEDGE BASE

In my experience, a common mistake new teachers make is to try to build skills like logical reasoning to improve pupils' writing before they have the strong knowledge base in the topic they are studying. Cognitive scientist Daniel Willingham reasons that logical thinking and problem solving are 'intertwined with knowledge, and one cannot deploy thinking skills effectively without factual knowledge' (Willingham, 2010). In line with this school of thought, if we want our pupils to be able to fully analyse the impact a subsidy will have on correcting a positive externality, they first need to have a comprehensive understanding of market failure, externalities, and the price mechanism.

Broad specifications mean there is a vast amount of information pupils need to remember. One of our goals, therefore, is to support pupils in remembering all this information, and this is where retrieval practice can be a game changer.

A lot of the work of teaching is about explaining concepts in such a way that the information makes it into pupils' heads. Retrieval practice asks to refocus on the opposite: getting information back out. Mark Enser describes it as 'retrieving something from our mind so it is easier to recall in future' (Enser, 2019) and this has been cited as the most effective revision technique (Dunlosky *et al.*, 2018).

The important thing about retrieval is that pupils are not looking at any notes. Instead, they are trying to remember information that they have been taught previously. A study by Karpicke and Roediger showed that pupils who attempted retrieval practice achieved '21% better marks on assessments than those who simply re-read notes to study' (Karpicke and Roediger, 2008). As odd as it may sound, the process of trying to remember actually strengthens memory. This is because remembering something we have previously learned is hard work, and we tend to remember what we have to really think about. Remember Willingham: 'Memory is the residue of thought' (Willingham, 2010).

BUILDING CHAINS OF REASONING

A feature of deep understanding in economics is being able to explain the impact a factor will have on an economy. A helpful analogy here is that we want pupils to understand an impact like dominoes falling: one falling leads to another falling, which causes another to fall and so on. For example, we want our pupils to understand that an effective advertising campaign can lead to higher demand for a good. This initially leads to excess demand and leads firms to increase the price of the good. Firms that supply the good then have a greater incentive to do so, so supply increases. This increases firms' profits and producer surplus, which in turn entails higher government receipts in corporation tax, which can be used to improve public services.

This sequence of events is called a 'chain of reasoning' (a skill that is required by all economics specifications and qualifications). In my experience, it is often the case that pupils will struggle to understand what a chain of reasoning is and often view the impact of a business decision as binary, like in the following common exchange I have with pupils:

TEACHER: What effect will a fall in consumer incomes have on business X?

PUPIL: The business will have lower demand if customers have less disposable income.

TEACHER: Good, and what is the impact on the business of this?

PUPIL: The business will fail.

One of our first tasks is therefore to explain to pupils what a chain of reasoning is. In my experience, pupils can quickly memorise connectives such as 'as a result of' or 'this means that' to connect different points together, but understanding the purpose of a chain of reasoning is the true foundation on which they can build this skill.

I like to introduce the idea by showing a video clip from *Toy Story*. Woody drives a remote-controlled car into a wall, which sets off a sequence of events that eventually leads to Buzz Lightyear falling out of the window. First, I ask my pupils to write down every single step between the car hitting the wall to Buzz falling out of the window. Then, I ask them to explain why each step leads to the next step. Whenever I discuss chains of reasoning thereafter, I continuously refer back to this analogy, asking pupils 'what happens next' and crucially reminding them to tell 'each part of the story' when they make large leaps.

A helpful technique as we teach a new topic is to ask pupils to fill in a table in which they are periodically prompted to complete the next link in the chain so that their minds are focused on exactly what the next step should be. Initially, I give mine prompts in brackets as extra scaffolding, and I gradually withdraw them over time so that they eventually complete the work independent of any external support (Sherrington, 2017). When pupils complete this work, I can give instant feedback on their chains by showing correct answers on the board, from which they can make corrections if necessary.

I do this for every topic, so that it quickly becomes a routine. It's a time-efficient resource which requires almost no prior planning, and pupils can either copy the resource into their exercise books or be given a print-out to fill in. I use the same template for a variety of different topics, and on those occasions where there is more than one correct answer, I go through a variety of possible answers to ensure they do not mark correct answers as wrong.

EXTENDING CHAINS OF ANALYSIS

A common problem I initially encounter is that pupils end every chain with 'and therefore the business has higher profit' or 'as a result, price and quantity increase'. The key here is to ensure your pupils can extend their chains of reasoning beyond simply talking about higher or lower profit and/or the impact on real GDP and inflation.

To this end, I amend some of my resource by filling in some links in the chain for pupils, and stop where the chain says 'therefore there will be an increase in profit' so that it is clear that I expect them to think beyond this point. While this appears to be a form of scaffolding, in fact it increases the level of challenge because it forces pupils to extend their chains of reasoning beyond profit as the final outcome.

You can even make it a rule in your classroom that no chain can end with higher or lower profit!

BUT, BECAUSE, SO

Because of the sheer breadth of content in economics, it is easy to fall into the trap of testing pupils' knowledge by vacillating between tables of information and short-answer quizzes on one hand and long essays on the other. An excellent way to bridge this divide and ensure pupils are adept at manipulating content and information is the 'but, because, so' technique explained in *The Writing Revolution* (Hochman and Wexler, 2017).

Pupils are given an extract to read and are then given the same statement, this time ending with 'but', 'because' or 'so' to prompt them to explain what has happened, why it has happened or the limitations of this. History teachers in particular have made excellent use of this technique and shared their resources publicly, for which we can all be grateful. This example from curriculum leader for history and education blogger, Kristian Shanks of a statement and its expected answers gives a good sense of its power:

1. Germany was unstable after the First World War because... *of the impact of the Kiel mutiny.*

2. Germany was unstable after the First World War but... *the new government was still able to survive the crises of this period.*

3. Germany was unstable after the First World War so... *the Spartacists took the opportunity to launch an uprising against the government (Shanks, 2020).*

So much of economics is about explaining why an event is happening and in what circumstances it might not take place. This technique can be a very effective tool in developing pupils' thinking and their sentence construction. As a result, they will be better equipped to construct longer paragraphs with appropriate nuance. For example, following an extract about failings of UK train operators, pupils can be set the following stimulus:

1. The government nationalised the East Coast rail line because... *of failings of private rail operators to provide an adequate service that is in consumers' best interests.*

2. The government nationalised the East Coast rail line but... *the majority of rail operators are still run privately.*

3. The government nationalised the East Coast rail line so... *this suggests that the private sector cannot efficiently produce services within a natural monopoly.*

These can be used for almost any textbook extract and can be a useful bridge between learning content and explaining it in a piece of extended writing.

EFFICIENT WAYS TO PRACTICE EXTENDED WRITING

While Malcolm Gladwell's famous claim that it takes 10,000 hours of practice for someone to become an expert in a skill has been disproved, there is no doubt that extensive practice is required for pupils to master writing detailed chains of analysis.

At A-level, these are typically practised through 25-mark essays that take 30 to 40 minutes to complete, so there is a strict limit to how many can be completed in class or even for homework. Let's imagine pupils in microeconomics in year 12 have finished learning about government interventions that can correct market failures. They learn around eight policies, and in an essay they compare two of them. In order to write enough essays so that each policy has been discussed, they need to write – and we need to mark – four essays. If each one has to be practiced five times for relative mastery, this adds up to 20 essays, taking up around 10 hours of lesson time.

As pupils' expertise develops, the important areas they need to be thinking about are what chains of analysis to use, what diagrams to include and how to link these to different stakeholders. Knowing this, to keep the challenge level high and the time usage low, I ask pupils to complete a substantial proportion of their essays 'in chains'. Instead of writing in full sentences, they briefly explain a link, draw an arrow and move onto the next one. This way, they still do all the hard thinking but can complete many more 'essays', practising a wider variety of questions.

Periodically, however, I still ask pupils to turn one of these into a full essay. This is so they don't forget the structure of essay, an economics essay or how to express their reasoning in full sentences and have opportunities to practice writing at length under timed conditions.

The topic of writing frames and set structures remains contentious among the profession. Some argue these restrict pupils' creative writing and ability to answer the question in front of them by forcing them to shoe-horn their thinking into a pre-allotted number of 'points'. I always provide a structure for how pupils should answer different types of questions. My experience tells me that this initial scaffolding actually helps pupils formulate their answers in a manner that ensures they tick off every assessment objective.

While it can make some answers appear slightly wooden, the objective is not for pupils to develop a discursive writing style appropriate for a newspaper (yet, though there's no reason to encourage those who can!) but to develop the economic analysis, application and evaluation to enable them to critically evaluate the hot economic topics of the day. In my view, a clear writing frame achieves these ends.

DEVELOPING PUPILS' VERBAL FLUENCY

Say it again, better

Having discussed a variety of ways to support pupils to develop their written chains of reasoning, we now turn to how to develop their general verbal fluency so that they can communicate using key economics terminology. This is critical in demonstrating understanding of the subject, and one way to achieve it is through ensuring all your pupils are prepared to answer any question you pose. When observing early-career teachers, I find they sometimes rely on pupils who put their hands up to answer a question. As explained in our earlier section on 'Keeping participation high', it is important not to do this, but to pick pupils instead. This technique of cold calling ensures all pupils who are prepared to answer a question are given the chance to practise verbalising their thoughts, and this approach helps you to assess their progress.

When pupils give an answer that is incomplete or doesn't use any or all the economics terminology it could, you can ask them to repeat their answer using accurate terms. This is known as 'Say it again, better' (Sherrington, 2017). You are giving pupils the time (and if necessary, the prompts) to improve their answer. For example:

TEACHER: In what circumstances would an increase in price increase a firm's revenue?

PUPIL: If there aren't many competitors so customers continue to buy from the firm despite the higher price.

TEACHER: That's correct, but say it again, better. Think about a key economics term you could use in your answer.

PUPIL: A lack of competitors means demand is relatively price inelastic so a higher price leads to an increase in a firm's revenue because demand reduces by a smaller proportion than the increase in price.

It is important to note that in this example the teacher specifies how the pupil can improve upon their answer, but this does not always have to be the case. In some instances, it's appropriate not to specify how an answer can be made better in order to encourage pupils to reflect for themselves on how they can improve. Of course, for some pupils this will not be appropriate and prompts may be required. As well as ensuring that your pupils can use accurate terminology in their answers, 'Say it again, better' also has the benefit of communicating the high expectations that you have of their verbal fluency in your lessons.

Pose, pause, pounce, bounce

Your pupils will quickly come to know that they cannot get away with using everyday language in your economics lessons, nor can they give half-thought-through answers. You can also involve other pupils in the process. Rather than telling pupil A whether or not their final answer is correct, you also have the option to bounce the question to pupil B and asking them if they agree with pupil A's answer and why. Ross Morrison McGill refers to this as 'Pose, Pause, Pounce and Bounce' (Morrison McGill, 2011). Pose a question, pause to give pupils time to think, then pounce by cold calling. Lastly, bounce their answer to another pupil for agreement/disagreement or additional detail.

Using 'Pose, pause, pounce, bounce', another way to develop pupils' verbal literacy is to play a game where pupils must give the next step in a chain of analysis. In order to ensure that pupils do not skip any links in the chain and are able to communicate every step in a logical manner, if a pupil misses a link, they are out. The game continues until there are no links left in the chain. (Or no students left to fill them in, but hopefully this is very rare!) For example:

TEACHER: What is an impact of a subsidy for education?

PUPIL 1: Firms have an increase in profits.

PUPIL 2: This means that they have an incentive to supply more.

PUPIL 3: This means there is no longer a market failure.

TEACHER: Sorry pupil 3 you are out! What should have been next in the chain?

PUPIL 4: Output has increased.

TEACHER: That's correct – before we get onto the market failure, we need to explain an increase in output. Only then do we discuss how the market failure can be resolved if the subsidy is equal to the external benefit.

This method supports pupils to learn how far they can extend their chains to explain the overall impact of a point, as well as understand the importance of not skipping any links in the chain when they are explaining their point.

DEVELOPING PUPILS' NUMERACY SKILLS

It is likely that your pupils will be involved in some form of business calculations when they leave education. For that reason, it is a common part of assessment for most business qualifications. (Under the new GCSE qualifications, 10% of marks are for quantitative skills.) So, it is imperative that your pupils have a strong understanding of the numeracy skills needed within business.

It's not untypical for teachers to provide pupils with an example of a business and then facilitate them in discovering calculations like profit and net cash flow themselves. However, research from John Sweller and others has shown that for novice learners, explicit instruction is a more effective way for pupils to learn new information than such minimally guided instruction (Sweller, Kirschner and Clark, 2006).

Building on that point, Barak Rosenshine's seminal work on instruction recommends an approach of gradually moving from worked examples and guided practice to full student independence (Rosenshine, 2012). In my experience, supported by this research, I find that the most effective way to teach calculations is the 'I do, we do, you do' approach to modelling (Sherrington, 2017).

Initially, I show my pupils exactly how calculating cross elasticity of demand is done, explaining each step of the process as I go. Following on from this, I give pupils a range of values with gaps to complete, and I go through the exercises with them. Finally, I give pupils an opportunity to complete independent work with no assistance, and only when this is completed do I provide them with feedback by putting the correct answers on the board. This is an easy activity for pupils to mark themselves as there is only one correct answer.

One of the biggest challenges for pupils is that there are often several different formulas to remember in order to complete calculations. Remembering that retrieval practice is the best way to ensure knowledge is retained, I create a weekly formula test for pupils to compete with no notes until I am confident that they remember all the formulas they need to know.

In economics, it is important not just to be able to complete calculations but to use the information to make appropriate decisions about a government policy (Sheedy, 2018). This means that it isn't sufficient for pupils to be able to calculate a firm's change in profits; they need to be able to use the information to show their critical thinking skills by identifying what measures the business can take to improve their liquidity, for example, and the impact on the efficiency of the market.

In order to develop this skill, it is crucial to bring quantitative skills into every topic you teach, regardless of whether pupils have to make a calculation. At every opportunity, pupils should be made to interpret data in order to make decisions about what the government should do in response to it. For example, when looking at market research, it's easy to include pie charts showing customer feedback with percentage values. Then, you can ask pupils to consider what actions the business should take with regards to launching new products in response to that feedback.

Quantitative analysis can be used in almost every economics topic, and it should be. What better way to ensure they have plenty of practice in interpreting data to make business decisions?

KEY POINTS

- Before pupils can develop effective economics paragraphs, they need a secure knowledge base which requires explicit instruction, clear modelling and feedback, and a large amount of retrieval.

- Create activities that specifically focus on building and extending pupils' chains of analysis.
- Connectives are central to building chains of analysis, and activities like 'Because, but, so' can be highly effective in developing this skill.
- Improving pupils verbal literacy is an important prerequisite for effective writing.
- All pupils can and should take part in activities that require them to express themselves verbally.
- Crucially, pupils should practice improving on their own and others' answers with activities like 'Say it again, better'.
- To maximise writing practice opportunities in a time-efficient manner, pupils can complete essay plans 'in chains'.
- Subject-specific numeracy skills require as much practice as subject-specific terminology.
- Opportunities for numeracy practice can and should be built into every topic.

REFERENCES

Agarwal, P. and Bain, P. (2019) *Powerful Teaching: Unleash the science of learning*. San Francisco: Jossey-Bass.

Birnbaum, M. S., Kornell, N., Bjork, E. L., and Bjork, R. A. (2013) 'Why interleaving enhances inductive learning: the roles of discrimination and retrieval', *Memory & cognition*. 41 (3), pp. 392–402.

Bjork, E. L., & Bjork, R. A. (2011) 'Making things hard on yourself, but in a good way: Creating desirable difficulties to enhance learning'. In: Gernsbacher, M. A., Pew, R. W., Hough, L. M. and Pomerantz, J. R. (Eds.) & FABBS Foundation, *Psychology and the real world: Essays illustrating fundamental contributions to society*. pp. 56–64. New York: Worth Publishers.

Christodoulou, D. (2016) *Making Good Progress? The future of assessment for learning*. Oxford: Oxford University Press.

Dunlosky, J. et al. (2013) 'Improving Students' Learning with Effective Learning Techniques: Promising Directions from Cognitive and Educational Psychology', *Psychological Science in the Public Interest* 14(1), pp. 4–58.

Fields, R. (2005) 'Making Memories Stick', *Scientific American*. 292, pp. 75-81.

Karpicke, J. D., and Roediger, H. L. (2008) 'The critical importance of retrieval for learning', *Science* 319(5865) pp. 966-968.

Kirschner, P., Sweller, J. and Clark, R. (2006) 'Why minimal guidance during instruction does not work: An analysis of the failure of constructivist, discovery, problem-based, experiential, and inquiry-based teaching', *Educational Psychologist* 41.

Lemov, D. (2015) *Teach Like a Champion 2.0: 62 techniques that put students on the path to college.* San Francisco: Jossey-Bass.

Rawson, K. A., and Dunlosky, J. (2011) 'Optimizing schedules of retrieval practice for duable and efficient learning: How much is enough?', *Journal of Experimental Psychology: General* 140(3) pp. 283–302.

Rosenshine, B. (2012) 'Principles of instruction: Research-based strategies that all teachers should know', *American Educator* 36 pp. 12-39.

Shanks, K. (2020). *Because, But, So — The 'washing hands' of writing? What I'm learning from TWR: Part Two.* [online] Avaliable at: https://kristian-shanks.medium.com/because-but-so-the-washing-hands-of-writing-what-i-m-learning-from-twr-part-two-f5685fabf3e8#/ (Accessed 21/02/2022).

Sheedy, K. J. P. (2018) *Good Thinking and Bad: Using the science of cognition to make better decisions.* Oxfordshire: Writersworld.

Sherrington, T. (2017) *The Learning Rainforest: Great teaching in real classrooms.* Woodbridge: John Catt Educational.

Willingham, D. (2010) *Why Don't Students Like School? A cognitive scientist answers questions about how the mind works and what it means for the classroom.* San Francisco: Jossey Bass.

REAL-WORLD APPLICATION

The great joy of teaching economics is that everything in it has a real-world application. There are no entirely abstract ideas and when you study economics, suddenly you understand the world in a way in which you never did before. And if that's not benefit enough, almost every decision we make can be better understood through the study of economics. I quoted John Maynard Keynes in the very first paragraph of my introduction, but it bears repeating: 'Practical men who believe themselves to be quite exempt from any intellectual influence are usually the slaves of some defunct economist.'

And yet, examiners' reports frequently highlight this area as a weakness. This is either in making developed chains of argument that relate to a specific industry mentioned in an extract, or pupils failing to utilise wider reading and their knowledge of real-world examples in their answers.

Pupils often make the mistake of thinking 'real-world application' is assessing their ability to quote an extract. They believe a relevant quotation will tick a box. However, application is a more detailed and nuanced skill of making economic arguments that are relevant to the specific industry or economy being discussed. In their A level schemes of assessment, all the exam boards describe application in economics in the same words. Assessment objective two (AO2) requires students to be able to 'apply knowledge and understanding to various economic contexts to show how economic agents are affected by and respond to economic issues'.

Yet, can pupils really be expected to know intricate details about every industry and country that they could potentially be asked about? How are they to have examples for every part of the specification? It is perhaps unsurprising that this is an area that so many struggle with. Luckily, there are a number of relatively low-effort ways to build students' practice so that they are able to make reasoned arguments that are applied to appropriate economic contexts.

UNDERSTANDING THE UK ECONOMY OVER TIME

In macroeconomics, an easy way for pupils to apply economic theory is to be familiar with the UK economy over time. I like to give a potted history of UK economic policy from the Second World War, which fits neatly into the A-level specification. When teaching fiscal policy and Keynesian economics, I talk through the increases in government expenditure during the 1960s and the post-war consensus. When we get onto the disadvantages of fiscal policy and its implications for an economy at its productive capacity, I introduce pupils to the increasing inflation of the 1970s (albeit with a nuanced discussion about its multiple causes) and the UK's IMF loan. Then, when we move on to supply-side policy, we discuss privatisation and deregulation during the Thatcher years, Gordon Brown's golden rules, Bank of England independence and the austerity years. This way, pupils can come to understand how the evolution of economic theory has influenced policy, and I provide them with a manageable number of real examples as we go. As well as these, it is important that students are aware of current trends in the UK economy too; for example, issues around British workers' productivity and the potentially precarious nature of work in the gig economy.

While this naturally lends itself towards macroeconomics, a history of economic thought can also enrich microeconomics lessons. Right at the beginning of most economics courses there is a discussion around the economic problem and then the price mechanism to explain how the market allocates resources. At this stage, I bring in a discussion around the industrial revolution and how it changed the way resources were allocated in the UK. I then move on to explaining the 'invisible hand' in Adam Smith's 1776 work, *The Wealth of Nations,* and the role self-interest has in a free market.

This is particularly important as it is something we can revisit when looking at the role of altruism when considering behavioural economics. An understanding of the working conditions in nineteenth-century industrial factories then places Marx's critique into context. Discussions around market failure then lead us to a look at Arthur Pigou's work on tackling externalities as well as how Elinor Ostrom disputed conventional wisdom around the tragedy of the commons*.

This might appear like some additional hinterland knowledge to engage pupils, but then we've seen how important that is. And actually, I would argue that, hinterland or not, it is fundamental. It is by understanding how economics has evolved and influenced world history that pupils can begin to see the economics in everyday life.

READ, READ, READ!
A balanced diet

Once pupils have an understanding of how economic thought has developed over time, they will need to take a more contemporary look at the subject. The beauty of economics is that almost everything in the news has some economics in it, so there is an abundance of articles pupils can read to broaden their understanding.

Remember Mansworth's *Teach to the Top*. We always ought to be considering what we want our students to be able to do when they reach undergraduate study. This isn't just about broadening their horizons, it's also about zooming into the detail of actions and consequences.

So, I try to give pupils a balanced diet of news articles from reputable news sources (usually *The Economist, FT,* BBC News and *The Guardian*), as well as academic journals to really push them. There is an active community of economics teachers on social media who often share relevant news stories. And websites like VoxDev, Econ Observatory and CoreEcon share a range of academic journals in a manner that is accessible for students.

One of the challenges is ensuring pupils are actually reading these without putting too onerous a demand on our workload. Sometimes, I ask pupils

---

*   The tragedy of the commons is an economic problem in which every agent has an incentive for and no barrier to consuming an available resource. As the resource is depleted, consumption harms all agents, yet none has any rational reason to stop nor to invest in replenishing the resource which others will continue to freely over-consume. The problem was first posited in 1883 by William Forster Lloyd with the example of shepherds' unregulated grazing on common land.

to answer comprehension questions which they leave out on their desk so that I can walk round and ensure they have completed them. Then we go through the answers as a class and the pupils self-mark. The disadvantage here will be immediately obvious to you: I am not able to assess the quality of each student's work. To negate this, I randomly take in one or two pupils' answers periodically. This keeps pupils on their toes and, assessed or not, they have all done more reading and comprehension than left completely to their own devices.

Finding the economics

While it is useful for pupils to build up an understanding of topical issues, it does not solve the problem of pupils struggling to understand how these relate to the economic theories they have been studying. This is what I call 'finding the economics'. In order to work on this skill, rather than actually asking pupils direct questions, I ask them to list economic theories or topics that are relevant to the article, as well as applicable diagrams. This typically requires a significant amount of modelling before pupils are ready to do it themselves.

The advantage is that pupils practice finding the links between a news story and economic theory, and the more they do this, the quicker they get at forming these links in their heads. This helps them directly with their ability to approach synoptic papers where they are expected to analyse the micro- and macroeconomic consequences of a policy.

Often, reading is categorised as 'additional work' and ancillary to the content pupils are learning. By this token, it is then treated as somehow immune to the retrieval practice needed for the rest of what pupils have to learn. However, we know that if pupils are going to retain knowledge in their long-term memory, they need to regularly practise retrieving the information at spaced intervals. This is no differencce for knowledge of real-world examples. In light of that, I include low-stakes quizzes for pupils to provide examples for different topics. For example, I might ask pupils to provide a statistic which shows how the UK railway system demonstrates that a privately-run natural monopoly may not be in consumers' interests. This ensures pupils remember the examples that they will need to recall in exams.

Often, I set entire quizzes purely about real-world examples relating to different topics. These are all, of course, based on examples that I have provided to pupils, so they should know all of them. This also serves as a useful check on how much pupils have been reading the texts I've set them. Sometimes, I tell pupils in advance that they will be given a detention if they do not get above a certain pass mark in a real-life examples quiz. I tell them what topics we will be covering so there is no chance pupils can get a detention for not understanding something – only be if they haven't read and memorised them.

Unsurprisingly, this proves to be a very successful way to motivate pupils to read their news articles. And it communicates quite clearly that reading is not 'additional' but core work!

PRACTICE DIAGRAM MANIPULATION

One perhaps under-discussed area of application is how to effectively manipulate diagrams. While this might not immediately appear as application, fundamentally pupils are looking at an extract and using it to alter a diagram. They are applying economic theory to a real-world example.

Pupils are likely to become adept at drawing supply-and-demand diagrams following considerable practice, but there are a number of diagrams that pupils can change in order to show their application. This is where the earlier example of asking pupils to draw potential diagrams on the basis of reading a news story becomes particularly useful. If there is greater demand for a particular firm, for example, rather than just drawing an outward shift in demand, pupils could show the change to average and marginal revenue curves to show the change in supernormal profit. Equally, a discussion on opportunity cost could be quickly shown on a production possibility frontier diagram. Almost any discussion around the labour market can be shown on a diagram.

This skill can also be developed by taking a diagram that pupils have learned and altering it. So, when discussing firms' ability to reduce pollution, pupils can show an inward shift of a marginal social cost curve to show a reduction in welfare loss. Or, pupils can learn the differences when drawing a natural monopoly diagram compared to a monopoly without high fixed costs.

Even simple things like showing inelasticity of demand or supply when drawing a shift can be a nice way to show application in a basic diagram.

The important caveat is that, to gain application marks, pupils need to explain why demand or supply is inelastic. They need to know this, and to that effect I always remind my pupils that 'this is not an art lesson'. It is not the diagrams themselves but the explanations that accompany them that gain credit for application in assessments.

As with most things, the best way to hone this skill is through practice. There are typically only a fixed number of ways a diagram is likely to be manipulated, so a large number of quizzes can help with this. Typically, I provide pupils with a one-line scenario and ask them to choose the diagram that will best represent it. Often, there is more than one diagram that pupils can choose from, so I ask them to draw as many as they think are relevant.

In examinations, being fluent in manipulating diagrams has the additional advantage of engineering efficiency. The more pupils practice them, the less they will need to think about them when they get to the exam. When answering a question, they will immediately know what relevant diagrams they can draw. Ideally, pupils should be able to go from reading an extract to drawing the relevant diagram(s) within 90 seconds.

USING DATA FOR APPLICATION

The one consistent message from examiners' reports across all economics qualifications and exam boards is the lack of data pupils use in their essays. I suspect part of the reason for this is that pupils have become so used to treating application as the insertion of a quote from an extract that they don't even stop to look at relevant data. That, and perhaps a lack of focus on numeracy throughout their course, which can only limit their sense of competence in its use.

At a rudimentary level, pupils need to ensure they are quoting data in their responses. As with anything in teaching, this is usually best taught through effective modelling. Initially, you can give pupils model answers that include data to back up the point being made. As you gradually remove this scaffolding, a verbal discussion when reading an extract will easily ensure pupils are analysing the data effectively.

In order to do this, pupils need a thorough understanding of what different values of data signify. This means they should be fluent on elasticity values, the difference between nominal and real values, the meaning of index linking *etc*. In order to test pupils on these, I like to use the multiple-choice questions from past papers as these often have a number of 'distractor' options that look right but are slightly incorrect to really test pupils' understanding of these quantitative skills.

Another important way that pupils can use data to ensure high-level application is to manipulate it in some way. When looking at a trend over time, pupils can show the difference in percentage change, for example. Another option is to show exports as a percentage of GDP. Another important caveat here: it should go without saying that whatever they do with the data needs to be relevant to their analysis. Pupils have a tendency to start shoe-horning data in everywhere after I have stressed the need for a greater level of data in essays! It takes a while for them to automatically ask themselves 'does this enhance the argument I'm making?' but it's worth the investment to make them better economists.

ANNOTATING MODEL ANSWERS

As discussed in our chapter on cognitive load theory, pupils benefit initially from a large number of model answers and worked examples so that they can understand how to construct their own. One important addition to this principle is that they also need to understand what makes these answers models and how they can replicate them. One effective way to achieve that is for them to annotate model answers to show where there is real-world application.

Initially, I model how to do this before then asking them to complete the activity themselves to see if they can spot where the application is. I sometimes use live modelling to that effect, writing a model answer on the board and asking pupils where the application is or how application can be added to the paragraph.

I also insist that pupils annotate the essays they submit for homework themselves. This is partly so that they continue to develop their own understanding of how these should be written but is also so that they can start to get into the right habits. By having to self-check if they have enough application (literally how many times they have annotated 'app' in their essays), they automatically get into the habit of considering application more in future attempts. This is a useful form of what some call metacognition, ensuring pupils are thinking about their own thinking – in this case, how they approach a piece of work.

THE GUMMY BEAR TEST

I like to apply the gummy bear test to pupils' essays. It's simple: I show a pupil's paragraph on the board, replace any mention of the relevant industry with 'gummy bears', and ask the class if the paragraph still makes sense. If it does, then the conclusion we invariably reach is that the paragraph was not specific enough. In other words, real-world application was not adequate. Initially, the gummy bear test can be passed by simply including a relevant quotation from an extract. However, in longer answers this becomes harder to do for each paragraph, forcing pupils to actively consider how they can make every chain of analysis specific to what they are considering.

For example, when discussing the difficulty in quantifying external costs when considering a Pigouvian tax to tackle climate change, pupils need to pass the gummy bear test by specifically referring to why loss of lives from droughts and rising sea levels are hard to place a monetary value on. Truly a point that will not apply to gummy bears!

While this is typically more useful for microeconomic questions, a similar strategy can be used for macroeconomics, whereby a random country is inserted to see if the paragraph still makes sense.

DEVISING YOUR OWN EXTRACTS

While almost any news article contains economics and there are many extracts from past papers to choose from too, from time to time it's necessary to select an extract to help pupils practice applying a specific economic theory. Some key considerations for selecting the best articles to use in extracts are:

- **The destination.** What are you and your pupils aiming for? It is important to consider precisely what it is that you want pupils to be thinking about. Ideally, this should include the use of academic language as well as synoptic thinking touching upon different aspects of the specification.

- **The topics covered.** Decide on the concepts at their core and then add to it. Given their complexity, case studies are excellent for summative activities and should provide plenty of details that link to additional concepts. Rigorous extracts provide information that gives pupils the opportunity to adopt a holistic approach by recalling and applying previously learned knowledge and skills.
- **Variety.** Provide a range of data and sources. Ideally an extract should have different viewpoints to enable pupils to compare the impact on different stakeholders. This should also include a mixture of data and text.

There is some crossover between economics extracts and case studies that are used in business classes. Ian Marcousé (1994) listed six tips for writing a case study which I find particularly relevant to devising extracts for my pupils. Here's how I've interpreted them:

1. Keep looking or thinking until you find the right story. It has to be engaging or cover at least cover a relevant and important topic, even if it doesn't make for inherently interesting reading.

2. Write your extract holistically, trying to give the business background as well as honing in on a specific theme. I am happiest when I've written a question that could be answered from multiple perspectives.

3. Look for a balance between words and data (graphical or numerical). Partly, this is to reflect business decision-making reality; and partly it's to give equal opportunities to those who think more clearly in numbers and in words.

4. Write the extract as a story and treat the questions as a separate matter. In other words, I don't have the questions in mind as I write. I want a 'true' story – not one that has been rigged to deliver questions!

5. Provoke a reaction. I want pupils to develop critical faculties – especially in a world where PR dominates business communication (including or especially corporate social responsibility) – so I choose materials accordingly.

6. Vary the questions. I like to have some open and some closed. The latter include numerical questions as well as written ones that are knowledge-based and restrict the possible answers (*eg.* 'Assess two

reasons why…'). The former have the scope and challenge to allow myriad right answers. They will typically be based on solutions to the featured company's problems, or development of their opportunities.

KEY POINTS

- An understanding of the evolution of economic theory over time helps students to relate their theoretical knowledge to real-world changes in the political consensus in the UK.
- Pupils can never read enough. As well as reading relevant, varied and balanced articles, they should be able to 'find the economics' and link sources to theories.
- Diagrams should be practised and manipulated in different ways.
- Regular quantitative skills questioning and modelling the use of data and diagrams in essays is crucial to integrating application of data in assessments.
- The annotation of model answers (including pupils' own work) is effective in developing their understanding of what application is and developing its habitual and relevant application.
- The gummy bear test helps students to understand where their answers lack specific real-world application and to improve their answers.
- When devising your own extracts, ensure they are relevant, holistic, balanced, narrative, provocative, and varied. (Sorry I don't have an acronym for you!)

REFERENCES

Keynes, J. M. (1936). *The General Theory of Employment, Interest and Money.* London: Macmillan.

Mansworth, M. (2021) *Teach to the Top: Aiming high for every learner.* Woodbridge: John Catt Educational.

Marcousé, I. and Lines, D. (1994) *Business Case Studies for Advanced Level.* London: Longman.

Smith, A. (2012) *The Wealth of Nations.* Ware: Wordsworth Editions.

EVALUATION

One of the trickiest assessment objectives in economics is evaluation. It means different things to different people, but in most specifications, evaluation refers to weighing up different perspectives to inform decisions.

The reason it's so often hard to teach is that critical thinking skills like decision-making are not standalone skills. In a famous study, Herbert Simon asked a novice and expert chess player to look at a series of different chessboard placements during a game and to then reproduce the pieces on a separate board from memory. He found that while the novice could only accurately reproduce five pieces, the expert player could reproduce two-thirds of the board (Simon and Chase, 1973).

This seems unsurprising. Of course, the expert chess player has better memory and cognitive ability – this is what makes him an expert player. The interesting aspect of this study came later, though. When the researchers repeated the experiment, this time with the chess pieces randomly scattered across the board, experts and novices performed equally poorly. The implication is that the expert's skill at remembering chess positions is due to having stored many entire games of chess in their long-term memory. The expert can remember and analyse a game of chess extremely well, but it does not transfer to other domains – not even to the very same chess pieces when they are not part of a game.

DOMAIN-SPECIFIC EVALUATION

The implication of evaluative skills being domain-specific is that, in order for pupils to be able to evaluate effectively, they need comprehensive knowledge of the economic concepts and theories they are being taught. Evaluation-specific lessons or exam technique lessons are unlikely to be effective. We often give pupils mnemonics for different methods of structuring evaluative paragraphs and essays. These aren't entirely without merit, but the fact of the matter is that there is no shortcut past a deep base of knowledge for making informed judgements.

This does not mean we are powerless at improving our pupils' evaluative ability. But to do that, we need to make it part of teaching each piece of content rather than a separate generic skill. For example, when teaching market failures, we need to consider what we want our pupils to know that will enable them to evaluate the impact of information asymmetry. We will need to teach about the effectiveness of government information campaigns to tackle information gaps, looking at relatively successful ones like drink-driving and vaccine hesitancy and less effective ones like blood donation. In that way, pupils can start to develop a nuanced view of how endemic information gaps can be.

Then, to understand the impacts on different stakeholders, we could look at the discovery that smoking has negative health and how the smoking market responded. (We might be more concerned about sugar these days, but the evidence base about Munchies is no match to that about Marlboros so I'm happy to leave that one to economics teachers of the future.) The discussion around attempts to block this information and analysis of rival advertising helps pupils evaluate whether consumers are rational enough to distinguish accurate and misleading information and also how large firms can use advertising to muddy the waters when full information would be detrimental to them. After that, a look at how fuller information about smoking has affected consumer and producer surplus and competing interests leads to discussion about the differences between information asymmetry and externalities. This last part ensures pupils understand that filling an information gap is not sufficient when consumers over-consume a good as they are disregarding the impact of their consumption on third parties, for example.

By this point, pupils are evaluating the impact of an information gap and in doing so they are able to consider whether it can be effectively filled by more information, its impact on different economic agents, whether it can be maintained through misinformation, how market failure might be reduced, and whether other factors are at play in causing it.

I go through this process for every topic. I start by asking what pupils need to know in order to make economic decisions, and then I teach it explicitly. I plan and sequence my pupils' learning in such a way that it leads them to build up the domain- and topic-specific schemas they need to evaluate effectively.

There is no shortcut, but this makes my teaching more efficient and effective. More of my students develop the evaluative skills they need, and I waste less time on standalone evaluation lessons that are more often than not too little, too late.

DECLARATIVE AND PROCEDURAL KNOWLEDGE

David Didau has written about an important distinction between declarative and procedural knowledge. Declarative knowledge refers to the 'things' I want pupils to know and procedural knowledge to what I want them to be able to do with it (Didau, 2019). If I want my pupils eventually to be able to solve problems about when governments should intervene in a market by imposing an indirect tax, the declarative knowledge they need includes:

- the market mechanism with perfect competition and without market failure
- the causes of market failure
- the comparison between market failure and perfect competition
- how an indirect tax can correct market failure
- the potential drawbacks of imposing this tax (ie, government failure)

This does not include the tacit knowledge experts use – often without realising it – when solving a problem. This needs to be automated with a strong retrieval strength so they are not having to think about this when problem solving. But what is that tacit knowledge? To understand that, we need to ask ourselves how experts and novices use information differently to process and solve a problem.

The key difference is that novices look at the superficial elements of a problem rather than the deeper structures at play. So, asked to evaluate if the government should impose a 'sugar tax' on fizzy drink manufacturers, they will focus on the problems caused by fizzy drinks rather than the deeper structure of negative externalities and government intervention that the question is really asking about.

When it comes to procedural knowledge, Didau identifies a problem he calls expert-induced blindness. We forget the steps we take to solve a problem – steps we learned as novices and have since become automatic for us. If we don't teach these steps, rather than consider the similarities between this problem and similar problems (which they clearly can't do as they haven't encountered many similar problems before), they look for other potential solutions by way of a means-end analysis.

The solution is schema acquisition: in other words, obtaining greater knowledge about the types of problems they will face and the types of solutions these require. The alternative, setting endless essay questions to practice with, will only see them fairly pointlessly devoting their working memory to means-end analyses.

Novices need to understand the steps we take to solve a problem: our procedural knowledge. Thankfully, our expert-induced blindness can be corrected. With a bit of thought, we can generalise the process by which we solve evaluation questions like the one about a sugar tax. Here are the questions we work through:

1. What is the difference between this situation and perfectly competitive markets?
2. What is its outcome (*ie*, What is the market failure?)
3. Which economic agents does this affect?
4. How would a tax correct this market failure?
5. Will the costs of imposing the tax be high?
6. Will the government be able to quantify the market failure to set the right rate of tax?
7. Will other non-economic incentives influence the rate politicians set?

8. Is demand for the product elastic or inelastic, and how does this impact the effectiveness of the tax?
9. Do the benefits outweigh the costs?

And there, quite simply, is a nine-step process to an effective evaluation. You could categorise steps five to seven together as 'government failure', but in my experience it's more effective to explicitly break the process down into its simplest steps.

The first step to teaching this process is to explicitly model how to address this problem. A novice learner requires a worked example here, so I provide my pupils with a case study that we read together, and from which I show my answers to the questions above.

The next step may be a partially completed answer. I give pupils a different news story to analyse, go through the first half of the questions with them, and leave them to attempt to answer the last few themselves with feedback. I repeat this exercise until I'm confident they can complete it effectively.

Then, they should practise this to the point of fluency, with opportunities for retrieval so that they can use this procedural knowledge to solve similar problems.

BEHAVIOURAL ECONOMICS AND ELASTICITY

I teach elasticities of behavioural economics early on in my A-level curriculum. One reason for this is that these become ready-made evaluations that pupils can use when considering the effect a change in demand or supply will have on a policy. When considering the effect of an increase in demand, I teach pupils to consider whether the change in price will really change demand if consumers are habitual, influenced by social norms or struggle to compute the changes, for example.

Similarly, they will consider if supply is likely to be inelastic in the short-term and how relevant this will be. I assess their ability to do this with targeted questioning as well as longer essays in which they must explain these points. It's worth reinforcing given how much of economics relates to a change in supply or demand. Understanding in detail how these factors can influence this is incredibly useful in enabling pupils to quickly evaluate the magnitude of a change in output or price. The aim is to do this so often that it becomes automatic by the end of the course. This becomes especially important given how tight most examinations are on timing. Sadly, one thing pupils don't really have time to do in their exam is think!

For macroeconomics, this works in a similar way. Much of what pupils are required to analyse relates to a change in aggregate demand. Pupils need to practise explaining how the impact of a shift in aggregate demand can change depending on whether the economy is at full capacity or not, and how this in turn affects inflation and unemployment. They also need to be able to explain the likely difference in the short term and long term. Then they must be able to explain how this could differ in classical and Keynesian models. And finally, to explain how the change in unemployment could vary depending on the level of mobility in the labour market.

None of these negates the need for more detailed, specific evaluations for every topic being covered. The purpose is simply to increase pupils' fluency in respect of the common types of evaluative questions that come up again and again because they are substantial components of the specification.

ECONOMIC AGENTS

Another common thread for economics evaluations relates to the impact of changes and policies on different economic agents. We looked earlier in this chapter at the importance of domain-specific evaluation, which calls for pupils to consider the impact on different agents for every topic covered. Initially, this can simply mean looking at how consumers, producers and governments are impacted. But this can (and should) eventually be taken a step further to consider how these interlink and how, for example, a negative impact on producers can go on to affect consumers through reduced innovation because less is spent on research and development.

Nor should producers be treated as a homogeneous block. There's the impact on competitors to consider, as well as suppliers and others in the production chain. And the same goes for consumers, who can be broken down into consumer groups with differing elasticities, for example. I make sure to explicitly teach the impact on different agents for every topic, and over time this routine means that my pupils get into the habit of comparing different agents even when I present them with an extract containing new information they have not been taught.

COUNTER-ARGUMENTS

Pupils often have the misconception that evaluation is simply listing a generic counter-argument to a point. The error here is only the over-simplification, but it is nevertheless a crucial element of evaluation. Teachers often worry that this is not 'real' evaluation and quickly skirt past it, but we should be drilling pupils to know and understand the advantages and disadvantages of different concepts.

I regularly and explicitly teach these and include them in quizzes in class and as homework. This is especially important for those big topics that are repeatedly assessed and act as a threshold to understand bigger economic concepts, including different government interventions to target market failure, fiscal, monetary and supply-side policies, different market structures and methods to increase economic development.

Evaluation is not just about counter-arguments, but knowing counter-arguments is foundational. All pupils must understand them in order to attempt more ambitious evaluation later, and it can never be practised enough.

QUESTIONING SOURCES

In our chapter on application, we looked at pupils' tendency to think of it simplistically as inserting a quote from the extract. Similarly, many often take what is written in an extract as gospel. An underused method of evaluation is to critique the bias of the source itself. Unsurprisingly, history students are often the most adept at doing this, but I always encourage pupils to look at who has written an extract and to consider whether this might mean there are potential biases to question. This is especially the case with quotes from a firm of industry body spokesperson.

A nice way to ensure pupils do this effectively is to spend some time teaching public choice theory. Spending time going through government priorities and why they may not necessarily be aiming to maximise the welfare of citizens can make it easier for pupils to question the motives of different economic agents.

As with anything, this is best done with modelling and practice, for example by taking an extract from almost any past paper and discussing who the source is and why they might be biased. This is typically not a detailed evaluation as there is not usually a great deal of analysis that can be made of it, but it can make a one-line evaluation as part of a wider point.

JUDGEMENTS

If evaluation is about making informed decisions, then the culmination of the skill is most evident in the final paragraph of longer economics essays, where pupils are expected to form a judgement about a government policy or the impact some decision or action will have. I provide a structure for pupils to cover three points in their recommendation.

The first is to fully justify the decision they have made and to ensure it answers the question. This can help structure the judgment as pupils sometimes end up off-topic towards the end of an essay. Then, I urge them to explain why their recommendation is accurate despite the evaluative counter-arguments they have made. This is crucial as the key to successful evaluation is to weigh up different arguments and explain why some points are more important than others.

The final part of the judgement is to explain what assumptions have been made or what the answer depends on. This is to show that nothing is absolute in economics and certain assumptions have been made to reach this judgement. This sentence often begins with 'It depends on...'

It is important to note that this is just a structure. While it is useful as a scaffolding for pupils, it is only effective if the other work in this chapter has been done so that pupils have the knowledge – declarative and procedural – to evaluate effectively leading up to that final paragraph.

As a final note, I find it effective also to avoid calling this final section a conclusion. The mere mention of the word tends to encourage pupils to summarise what they have already said rather than to weigh up their arguments and reach a settled judgement.

KEY POINTS

- Evaluation is not a generic skill but a domain-specific one, so evaluative strategies need to be explicitly taught in every topic.
- Much of what experts do happens unthinkingly (automatically) and needs to be teased out so that it can be made explicit to pupils.
- Significant practice on evaluating using concepts like behavioural economics and elasticity is needed as these can be used to evaluate a wide range of impacts.
- Pupils must practise evaluating impacts over different timescales and also on different economic agents.
- Evaluation is about more than counterpoints, but practising counterpoints for each topic is nevertheless foundational to good evaluation. Don't skim over it!
- Questioning the validity and bias of different sources and how much weight to give each type of evidence is a useful evaluative practice.
- There is no such thing as a conclusion, only a qualified settled judgement based on the evidence.
- Final essay paragraphs should justify a decision, explain its recommendations and acknowledge its limitations.

REFERENCES

Didau, D. (2019) *Making Kids Cleverer: A Manifesto for Closing the Advantage Gap.* Carmarthen: Crown House Publishing.

Simon, H. and Chase, W. (1973) 'Skills in chess'. *American Scientist.* 61, pp.394-403.

CURRICULUM

Economics is not on the national curriculum. It is an optional subject at GCSE and the reality is that few schools offer the subject at key stage 4. The majority of students who follow A-level economics encounter the subject for the first time in year 12. Consideration for how to teach the subject and sequence pupils' learning so that they will have the knowledge, understanding and application to become, at the very least, economically literate citizens, is about so much more than preparing them to jump through examination hoops at the end of year 11 or year 13. Examination success is a by-product of educating students about economics, rather than the main objective.

Curriculum has become a hot topic in education, but conversations often revolve around key stage 3. Economics teachers sadly tend to have little input into that, and the result is a tendency to think of the economics curriculum as largely determined by exam specifications. The amount of content to be taught in the allotted time means consideration for what pupils should be taught, how and in what order is often sidelined. In my view, we are subject experts and it is our role to consider the optimal order for communicating our subject. Exam boards are assessment specialists. We are teaching specialists. These are different domain-specific skills and we should embrace ours.

THE PURPOSE OF AN ECONOMICS CURRICULUM

The core question we want our students to grapple with in economics is what we call the 'economic problem': If there are not enough resources to satisfy all wants, what is the best way to allocate those resources? It is a question that sounds remarkably simple to non-economists, but we want our pupils to understand the complexities entailed in answering it. They are, after all, the kinds of complexities that mean different answers have started wars and sparked revolutions!

We, therefore, want our student economists to appreciate the extent to which the government or the market should lead in allocating resources. I like to bring in some historical context at this stage, going through a timeline that starts with pioneering economist Adam Smith and threads through Bolshevism, the post-war consensus in the UK, Thatcherism and the Occupy movement that followed the financial crash. This is the hinterland knowledge of economics we talked about earlier, and it helps to give economics students an understanding of why what they are learning matters. It enriches the core content, and makes the real-world application of the subject palpable.

Next, in order to effectively answer our core question, pupils need to at least have a sense of what is both the most efficient and the most equitable way to allocate resources. In my experience, they need to be able to think about that on three levels.

At the individual level, how do we choose who gets what effectively? So, for example, is it reasonable for me to get this mobile phone when others can't due to lack of disposable income? Is there a better way to operate the economy that can increase equity without losing efficiency, or is losing efficiency a price worth paying for a more equitable society?

At the national level, how do we decide who gets what income? This is the start of our thinking about macroeconomics, but it leaves the core purpose of the curriculum unchanged. All that is really happening is that we are using the economic problem as a lens to examine and explain a nation's resources rather than those of individual firms or consumers.

Finally, at an international level, why is it that people in certain nations are residually wealthier than others? What role does the market or the government have in allocating resources at a national and global level?

The reason that economics is so important – and would we teach it if we didn't believe it was the most important thing we could do? – is that it explains so much of how the world works. Students need the economic tools to analyse those three layers to get even close to tackling the economic problem.

CURRICULUM SEQUENCING

Microeconomics

The very first thing to ask your pupils is very simple: 'What does 'scarcity' mean?' Or to put it even more simply: 'Why can't we all just have everything?' From that arises our exploration of whether the market could fix that problem. Now that pupils know what they are supposed to be answering, they will need to understand the concepts of demand and supply, which underpin everything in the market and help us to understand how it allocates scarce resources. It is necessary to constantly revisit this because the causes of shifts in supply and demand can appear abstract. It is imperative that pupils understand that this is a tool to explain how resources are allocated, not a discrete topic but a vital part of answering that wider question: 'Why can't we all just have everything?'

Students need to have a solid understanding of what these concepts mean before you explore how demand and supply interact to allocate scarce resources. Most specifications insist on using diagrams to 'analyse demand and supply'. They introduce the idea that where demand and supply are equal a market reaches an 'equilibrium' point which determines the price of a product and the quantity demanded and supplied at that price. The trouble is, that analysis is not explicitly linked to the economic problem. The whole point of explaining the interaction of demand and supply is that it is at the heart of the way markets operate. And the free market – where there is no government intervention and demand and supply determine price and quantity – is one possible way to allocate scarce resources. The market mechanism is one solution to the economic problem: to let the market forces of supply and demand determine how resources are allocated.

At this point, we can re-introduce some of the economic history we presented initially and succinctly as hinterland knowledge to drive pupils' understanding of the subject's purpose. Now pupils have enough economic knowledge that they are able to understand that history more richly. They can make sense of Adam Smith's 'invisible hand': how the hidden forces of the market lead to the most efficient allocation of resources, even when everyone is acting in their own self-interest.

At this point, we have answered our economic problem. Resources are scarce so they need to be allocated; the free market allocates resources through the price mechanism; therefore, a market free of state intervention will lead to an efficient allocation of resources. When pupils are entirely secure with this analysis of how markets operate, more complexity can be introduced to show why this might not always be the case.

Now is the time to ask whether there are circumstances under which the market does not lead to an efficient allocation of resources. Why might the market not work? That leads on to the economic concept of 'market failure'. It's important that at this stage this remains a very technical analysis. It's too early to talk about inequality or unfairness. We are merely enquiring as to why the market is not leading to efficient allocation. Students must first understand why the market does not work, so that they can fully justify their opinions about the ethics of market failure later. A common criticism of economics curricula is that they focus on technical market failures instead of more moral questions. These critics read into this a bias towards a neoliberal paradigm. However, our role as economics teachers is to explain the technical analysis of markets and why they fail and point pupils towards arguments (both positive and normative) about the role of markets, rather than to push any particular political perspective in the classroom.

Before getting into the details of market failure, I start off by introducing behavioural economics as one reason why the price mechanism may not lead to an efficient allocation of resources. I do this a lot earlier than many exam specifications suggest because I think it is useful for pupils to start to engage in the debate about economic models and to question the accuracy of their assumptions. Not only does this provide a useful critique of what they have already learned, but it also means they are exposed early to some of the criticisms of economics as a discipline and whether it deserves to be considered a science. This is a topic that can be returned to throughout their time on the course.

Now that pupils have an understanding of how the market should lead to an efficient allocation of resources and why alternative views of consumers' rationality and elasticities of supply and demand might prevent this, they can consider technical market failures. Even if it is not on the specification you are teaching, I highly recommend teaching the 'tragedy of the commons' at this stage. As well as being an incredibly important concept, it also provides pupils with an intellectual economic understanding of climate change and enables them to engage in these debates.

Once pupils have an understanding of why markets should lead to an efficient allocation of resources and why and when they fail to do so, the obvious next step is to ask about alternative ways to allocate scarce resources. Our questions will include: What are the benefits and drawbacks of intervention at an extreme level with a completely state-run, centralised economy, or at a Scandinavian-style level of mixed economy? How might these work? How can these fix market failure?

We have the economic problem. We have the market solution. We have market failure. How can the government fix that market failure? It is really that simple in economics. And the hinterland knowledge to bring back in at each stage is evident.

The next step is to point out that government intervention can fail too. Because, ultimately, in economics everything fails. From there students can begin to form a view on the best way to allocate resources. If we accept the market does not always work effectively, and government intervention is not always going to work either, we cannot hold polarised views because there are numerous examples of success and failure on both sides. You then deepen knowledge and understanding to the point where students begin to form their own answers to questions such as: 'What is the best way to govern?' and 'What is the best way to manage an economy, if it can be managed at all?' But students cannot begin to contemplate answering these questions and thinking like economists until they securely understand those five building blocks:

- The economic problem
- Demand
- Supply
- The market
- Government intervention

Once they have, they can start to look in more depth at how different markets operate by introducing differing market structures, labour markets and inequality. All of this has the same purpose, though: understanding the economic problem and different ways resources can be allocated.

Macroeconomics

The principles and sequence I've just outlined for microeconomics work just as well for macroeconomics. Start by looking at consumers and businesses. Take it a step further to government activity at a national level and exploring measures such as unemployment and inflation. Then it's just another step to looking at the international level and concepts like globalisation. But it must begin at a very basic level, establishing how economic agents interact, and only gradually expanding further and further before tackling the huge problems of poverty, famine and climate change that we all want to grapple with.

Harking back to that Keynes quote you have already read twice in this book, my view is that learning economics lifts the blindfold on the way our world is organised. When someone on the news talks about immigrants stealing domestic jobs and depressing wages, or claims that raising unemployment benefits encourages joblessness, or tells us about the dangers of carbon dioxide emissions, all those issues are actually related to fundamental economic questions. Understanding economics unlocks the door to understanding so many problems in the world.

One of the dangers of economics as a subject is that it can feel as though we teach a lot of separate topics. One day, we are talking about monopoly, the next about elasticity of supply. And if it is not always obvious to us how these are linked together, what chance do our students have of making those links? Curriculum sequencing that starts with hinterland knowledge and stretches logically through to broader and broader questions helps to show the 'golden threads' that connect these different topics – and they all start with the knotty economic problem.

A very broad question like 'Should we leave resource allocation to the markets?' is a way to link together many different topics. Economics is quite diagram- and calculation-focused, and this is one of the reasons that there is a real danger students will stop seeing the links between topics.

These broad questions reveal a lot of territory that can take us usefully into other discourses. You can link economics to politics or religion, even to psychology or sociology, or host of other disciplines and discourses.

Taught this way, economics creates an ongoing story that is built sequentially, where the students delve into substantive, important ideas. There is a kind of coherence which is deeply satisfying for students and teachers.

But 'big questions' doesn't necessarily mean 'global' or 'abstract'. It's important also to consider our school communities and how economics lends itself to answering their questions. I think of this most when teaching labour markets. I teach in a London school where many children are either the children or grandchildren of migrants. In terms of their world, topical discussions about immigration can trigger such emotional reactions on all sides. It is important to me that my students, when they hear comments about immigration on the news, have a deep understanding of its economic context.

But this can't be about promoting a particular view of immigration or policies relating to it. I want my pupils to form their own. We talk a lot in society about tackling bigotry and xenophobia. Fine, but it is important for me that when my students finish my economics course, they do not merely campaign politically from a moral standpoint alone. If they have an intellectual understanding of the economic reality of immigration, it will only help them make their case and better understand what is going on in the world as they grapple with their own identities. It is important that economics enables my students to make sense of themselves and to navigate some of the challenges that all of us who are children of immigrants face.

It is why I always go further than most exam specifications and analyse in detail the impacts of immigration on the labour market. I include more recent economic analyses from economists like Esther Duflo to show empirical evidence relating to immigration's impact.

Our students' economic education must not stop when they leave the classroom. There is a real point to this subject, and it reaches far beyond just markets and finance.

DEVELOPING CURRICULUM MATERIALS

The benefits of sequencing

I have constructed a booklet for each topic in economics. When writing those booklets, I thought I knew a lot about the subject, but the process led me to realise I needed to know more so that I could better distil the subject's essence for my students. The more you know, the more you realise how little you know, and the more challenging it becomes to decide what is essential and what is not. So, my booklets are consistently improving; in the meantime the students find them helpful, and not least because they are structured in a way that gives a clear sense of the narrative of economics as a subject.

Take 'comparative advantage' which, in a very simple sense, allegedly shows how everyone benefits from trade regardless of your starting position. It is, however, a very complex term to understand. It involves a lot of diagrams. It is illustrated through mathematical examples. When I was writing a booklet about trade, I had to work out how to break down 'comparative advantage' step by step before I could be confident my work would result in the students getting an overall understanding of the concept (and a comparative advantage over students without my booklet). It is a difficult thing to do.

When I was writing questions on the component parts, it tested myself on how deeply I understood the topic. This wasn't so much about revealing what I didn't know (though that helps too) but whether I was able to break down these economic concepts into the kind of bite-sized components students need to build up gradually to this quite complex and important theoretical term. A lot of the material in the resulting booklets is the material that I used to develop my own understanding. And what makes it accessible to my pupils is the order it is presented in.

Which is to say that the very act of planning the booklets is incredibly useful professional development in itself. I have had to think deeply about how to explain something, how to break it down to its constituent parts. And the result ensures that the students are doing lots and lots of practice. The questions are already written down beforehand, and the precise wording of the questions is helpful. With a booklet, all the material you need is in one place, and the students can see the whole journey because a booklet might include anywhere up to 300 questions, deliberately sequenced. They can see how we gradually build towards answering fundamental economic problems.

Narrative links

One of the challenges facing economics students is that there is no definitive answer to most questions. There are always advantages and disadvantages to a policy decision. For example, how effective is a government policy to minimise pollution, as pollution is considered a failure of the market? So, should we tax carbon? Should we give subsidise to wind farms? Should we have a tradable permit scheme like the EU have? And how do we choose the best policy?

You can teach students each policy explicitly and then draw upon real-life examples of when they have worked or not worked. The danger is that it is all too easy to expect students to infer all this by themselves. There is a tendency to approach these evaluative questions as though students require some kind of spark of genius to work it out. In truth, we have 500 years of economic examples to draw upon of policies that worked, or failed, or worked and then eventually failed. We teachers have delved into that half a millennium our entire careers, and however long – early-career teacher or seasoned old hat like me – it is a lot longer than our pupils.

But as important as making these links is, there is a pretty hard limit to how much we can impart in the time we have. An often-untapped source of relevant knowledge resides in the links between our subject and others our students are sitting: politics, geography and history, psychology and sociology, not to mention maths and English.

How can we improve our links with these? And how can we do it coherently? Adam Smith's concept of the free market was a great argument against slavery; Smith was convinced we could become wealthy through trade and not through bondage. It's useful to know what pupils have been taught about this in their history lessons or through the study of literature, for example. Not only is there opportunity for spaced repetition across the curriculum here, it is deeply satisfying for students to make those connections; people love making connections.

Recently, looking at what Marx wrote about capitalism and trying to put it into context for my students, I remember saying something like, 'Well, OK, it might seem clearly false now, but actually if you put it into context and know the factory conditions in Manchester where Engels and Marx were, we can understand, maybe, how it felt.' It was only months later that I realised that my pupils had studied a whole segment on the industrial revolution in history. They had a genuine understanding of what poverty and inequality meant in the country at that time. It was a golden opportunity to make my teaching and my students' understanding of the topic much richer than it was. It went begging that time, and it won't again.

In the end, it's all about narrative. I love the stories in economics. I think so much of history is economic history. For example, you might ask, 'How did the great depression completely alter our understanding of economics?' You can't really understand Keynes without understanding the class system. And if you have ever taught World War II, you know how important the great depression is considered to be as a determining factor. But if you don't understand the great depression, you can't really understand the OPEC oil price spikes of the 1970s or supply-side economics. And if you don't understand the miners' strike, you don't really understand the impact of Thatcherism on the UK economy and you can't really make sense of New Labour's attempt to appear economically moderate, which leaves you with little to draw on to wrap your head around the banking crisis of 2008.

There are so many of these historical nuggets that make economics make sense. And so many economic nuggets that make history make sense. Unpacking the curriculum like this enriches our understanding of curricular depth and power (even if it does not literally translate into something within a work scheme).

KEY POINTS

- The core purpose of any economics curriculum is arm students with the knowledge and tools to give nuanced answers to the economic problem of allocating scarce resources.

- A brief history of modern economic thought about this problem provides a useful introduction and framework for contextualising the curriculum journey.
- Students will need to think about the core problem on three levels: local, national and international.
- Separate curriculum sequences are necessary for micro- and macro-economics, though their overlaps should also be mapped out so that opportunities for cross-referencing are not missed.
- The five building blocks of the microeconomic curriculum are the economic problem, demand, supply, the market and government intervention. They should be introduced in that order and each securely grasped before moving to the next.
- The principles for sequencing macroeconomics are similar, starting from the economic problem, but this time looking at agents – first consumers and businesses, then governments and onto supranational organisations and globalisation. Tackling huge problems like climate change is the culmination of that sequence.
- Big questions are not necessarily global in scale. Local labour market problems can be just as complex in terms of economic analysis (and sometimes more meaningful).
- Creating booklets for each topic not only results in a rich resource and source of questions for students to practice, the act of breaking down concepts and sequencing them in this way is a very effective exercise in professional learning.
- Students don't need a spark of genius but a large store of examples to draw on in order to improve their evaluative skills.
- Creating a curriculum narrative from hinterland to current affairs helps to embed these examples.
- Seeking out cross-curricular links can also be a rich source of further narrative links.

HOMEWORK

When I first started teaching, my school policy was to set three hours a week of homework for A-level pupils and one hour a week for key stage 4. I attempted a variety of different homework tasks to engage pupils. To motivate them to do it I made sure to mark each piece of work, which very quickly became impossible.

Concerned that this wasn't stretching pupils enough, I attempted instead to set a multitude of essays each week for pupils to complete. As well as creating an unmanageable workload, it also meant that pupils were not getting the consolidation of knowledge they needed. They certainly weren't fully benefitting from the spaced practice we know to be effective.

Based on some years now of trial and error, and backed by the research we have looked at throughout this book, I have narrowed down what pupils need for effective homework in economics to four tasks:

- Regular retrieval practice
- Reading topical news articles
- Practising essay writing
- Answering data response questions

Optimally, work set should be effective in terms of improving pupils learning while avoiding an onerous marking workload. Let's look at each of these in turn...

REGULAR RETRIEVAL PRACTICE

As we discussed in detail in our earlier chapter, pupils need to practise recalling knowledge from memory at regular intervals to get past the 'forgetting curve'. Knowing this, I set retrieval quizzes as homework twice a week. Each task contains 30 questions that cover a range of topics taught over the entire course.

It's easy to keep workload down with these. There are a number of websites that can assist: Teams, Microsoft Forms and Google Forms can be used to great effect. You can even get software to mark quizzes for you. I like to use Carousel Learning. Pupils complete the questions and then are given the answers so that they can self-mark. I only have to make sure they have done the last bit accurately and collate information common errors.

I will then use this information to re-teach if necessary, and ensure the questions are repeated in a 'Do now' or further homework quiz at a later date. The challenge is that retrieval should really be done from memory, and there is no way of ensuring pupils at home are not looking at their notes. The best way to tackle that is to clearly explain the benefits of retrieval, and to ensure students know these tasks are as low-stakes as can be.

This also helps increase pupils' motivation. The more quizzes they do, the more they see their benefit as their retrieval strength grows. It's a low-maintenance and extremely positive feedback loop.

READING NEWS ARTICLES

As discussed in the chapter on application, it is important that pupils regularly read widely to understand how economics applies in the real world. I set some reading weekly. Don't stop at setting a news article for pupils to read, though. Ask them to do something with it. Sometimes I ask them to answer comprehension questions, but more often I will ask them to complete a pro forma in which they are required to explain what economic theories link to the article and/or pull key quotes and applicable diagrams from the text.

This serves the purpose of ensuring pupils are selecting the relevant parts of the article for their notes to aid with exam revision while also gaining practice in developing the links between different topics. I ask pupils to leave their completed pro formas on their desk so I can have a cursory glance during the lesson to ensure they have done it and then give feedback to the whole class so they can self-mark.

This activity can be challenging given that multiple answers are possible, but this can form part of a structured class discussion. This way, pupils are held to account for their work, get the opportunity to verbalise their opinions, and my marking workload stays mercifully manageable.

ESSAY WRITING

There's no avoiding it altogether: students must also practise their extended writing, and it simply can't all be done in class. I therefore weekly set either one essay in full or three or four essays 'in chains' as discussed previously. This way, pupils are still being asked to consider a holistic question that stretches them, as well as writing under timed conditions.

These are typically questions obtained from past papers. The content is largely similar across exam boards, so I will often use questions from different exam boards. And if there is a particularly topical issue or a challenging question that I can think of (and there often is) then I write my own.

As pupils become more confident in this, I focus on the most challenging essay questions. These are either questions that are very specific so they really test pupils' knowledge of a subject, or at the opposite extreme, so vague that they really require pupils to consider the links between different topics.

I will read through these and provide whole-class feedback, but I will not typically mark these individually. I have no guarantee they were completed under timed conditions no matter how earnest I am in asking them to, which nullifies their validity as an assessment.

DATA RESPONSE QUESTIONS

Data response questions give pupils valuable opportunities to practise answering questions about extracts. There is a plethora of these on old specification past papers, and they can easily be tailored to recent specifications.

The benefit of these over essays is that they are usually more specific, so they are a good test of pupils' understanding of a broad range of topics. Some exam boards expect pupils to evaluate even in low-mark questions.

By doing one of these a week, pupils can very quickly build fluency in that particular skill.

Some argue that this is a failing of some specifications. What is considered here as evaluation is really just a one-line counter-argument. Perhaps, but it remains a requirement in pupils' final examinations nonetheless, and as discussed earlier, the practice is incredibly useful for other aspects of the qualification.

I will typically take these in just to ensure they have been completed and, after a cursory glance, I go through model answers with the entire class, expecting them to make corrections as we go.

As with reading articles, this needs to form part of a class discussion given multiple potential answers.

While this all may seem like a lot of homework, a clear and consistent routine quickly become a habit for pupils. Different schools have different policies regarding the quantity of homework teachers must set, and you will work within those parameters, but the key criteria for effective homework in any subject is not the quantity, but the quality. A mixture of these tasks will ensure it.

KEY POINTS

- Four key tasks should make up the bulk of economics homework: regular retrieval practice, reading, essay writing, and answering data response questions.

- Homework can easily make teacher workload unmanageable, but clear routines and expectations can mitigate this.

- Regular retrieval practice can be easily managed with twice-weekly, 30-question quizzes that are marked automatically by software or self-marked. These also have the benefit of directly informing what the teacher needs to re-teach.

- Reading articles alone is insufficient; Students should have to do something with the information. Answering comprehension questions or completing a pro forma simply linking the reading to economic theories makes for work that can easily be marked in class.

- Essay questions for students to consider at home should grow in complexity over time, as their reliance on answering 'in chains' decreases. Whole-class feedback is ample, as there is no guarantee the answers have been written in timed conditions.

- There is a substantial back catalogue of data response questions to draw on, and while answering them is less challenging, it is a required skill in exams. Going through model answers in class is often sufficient by way of feedback.

COMMON MISCONCEPTIONS

There are some topics across micro- and macroeconomics that seem to trip pupils up every time. Below are some examples of common misconceptions I have noticed pupils making repeatedly, and some of the ways I go about teaching these topics to anticipate them and hopefully prevent these misconceptions from arising.

As with all teaching, there are no perfect answers here but this is how I attempt to incorporate some of the research around explicit instruction and cognitive load theory to explain complex economic topics.

MOVEMENT AND SHIFTS IN DEMAND

One of the early topics that often confuses pupils is the difference between a movement in a demand curve and a shift. This problem is exacerbated when some exam boards, having listed movements and shifts in demand curves in their specifications, then use terms like an 'increase in demand' in examination papers.

Most teachers will start by explaining how demand varies with price, explaining why there is an inverse relationship between the price charged and the quantity demanded. At this point, however, and before getting into diagrammatical examples, I ensure pupils have a comprehensive understanding by answering numerous practice questions about the relationship between price and demand and explaining exactly why demand falls when price increases.

Following this, I introduce a numerical example. True to my Scottish roots, I always use that how of demand for Irn-Bru changes dependent on price. I show five price points and show the difference in quantity demanded. I then model how this is drawn in a diagram and, crucially, label each price point on the diagram, showing that this is a movement along the demand curve. The point has *literally moved* along that curve.

After pupils practise drawing this diagram, they answer questions defining what a movement along a demand curve is and, importantly, explaining 'the *only* factor that can lead to a movement in a demand curve' to ensure they all understand that this movement only relates to price change.

I stick to the same example for the next bit, where I explain why an advertising campaign could lead to greater demand for Irn-Bru at every price point. The key point to emphasise is that this is occurring at every price point, and not *because of* price. I immediately ask pupils how this compares to a movement along the demand curve to ensure they are thinking about the difference. I then return to the numerical example, this time adding a column which pupils fill in to show the new demand, assuming the advertising campaign has led to an extra 5,000 sales at every price point.

Pupils plot this curve on the diagram they have already drawn and only now is the concept of a shift introduced. As the concrete example has been fully explained, it is now possible to go to an abstract definition and explain that a shift occurs when quantity of demand changes due to a factor other than price. I ask questions about this, and finally put a range of scenarios to pupils and ask them to determine whether they would cause a movement or shift in demand to ensure pupils fully understand.

As a tricky concept, I regularly revisit it through spaced retrieval practice in 'Do now' quizzes until I am comfortable it is firmly grasped. I follow the same process for movement and shifts in supply curves, although once demand curves are clearly understood, the process is less laborious.

DEFLATION AND DISINFLATION

As we saw in our chapter on explicit instruction, deflation and disinflation are often tricky concepts to distinguish between. I promised I would return to them in more detail, and here we are. Assuming inflation has already been taught, it is common for teachers to use numerical examples and introduce quantitative skills around percentage change to explain deflation and disinflation, but I would advise against this. For pupils without a strong understanding of percentage change, this can present significant extraneous cognitive load as they must understand exactly what decreases in percentage change mean, how they differ from a reduction in quantity and then apply this to economic concepts.

Instead, I start with the concrete example I told you earlier. Remember my nephew? I tell my students about how as a baby he was growing by as much as 10% each year, but as he gets older, he is growing by less. By the time he is my students' age, he will be growing by some 2% annually. My nephew has not shrunk and nor have they. They are simply growing at a slower rate. I show this on a diagram on a whiteboard as I go.

I'm not old enough to use myself as an example for the next bit, so I talk more generically about how as someone gets older, their height might actually reduce. I show this on a separate diagram to the right-hand side of the first, ensuring that I label each one. The one on the left shows disinflation, and the one on the right shows deflation. The advantage of this is that by attaching the terms to concrete examples, it is clear on a conceptual level what the terms mean. Pupils then need to answer questions to define both terms and to explain how they differ.

Only at this stage, once I am comfortable that pupils understand the difference between them, will I introduce numerical examples and ask pupils to determine whether these show deflation or disinflation.

A nice example to use to get quick whole-class feedback on this is to show a graph of a change in Japan's inflation rate over the past 40 years. Point to any given year and ask pupils to show you on their mini whiteboards whether it was a year of higher inflation, deflation or disinflation.

PROGRESSIVE AND PROPORTIONAL TAX

The first time I taught progressive and proportional tax systems, I explained both terms and the difference between them in around 60 seconds before moving on. In what I later learned to be a textbook example of the 'curse of knowledge', my strong understanding of the topic led me to lack empathy and understanding for how challenging it could be for novice learners. Every year, it is a topic that pupils struggle to differentiate between, and so now I carefully sequence my explanation.

I start by explaining what a progressive tax is. Rather than getting bogged down in irrelevant (for the moment) details about thresholds and to reduce extraneous load, I simply use the example of a person on a low income and one on a high income with the latter paying a higher tax rate. I call this a progressive tax and give a definition that emphasises the higher rate of tax paid as incomes rise. Pupils complete practice questions explaining the definition and looking at a range of examples explaining whether the tax is progressive and why.

At this point, I introduce the example of a country with the same rate of tax for all taxpayers. Initially, I use this as a non-example to further explain what a progressive tax is. I would use a numerical example of someone earning £20,000 paying 10% tax (so paying £2,000) and another person earning £200,000 also paying 10% tax (so paying £20,000). We ascertain why this isn't a progressive tax despite the higher earner paying more. Once this is clear, I explain that this is an example of a proportionate tax.

Finally, pupils explain both definitions, how they are different from each other, and explain whether the numerous examples of tax systems I present them with are progressive, proportionate, or regressive.

PRICE ELASTICITY OF DEMAND

The concept of elasticities is often introduced straight after demand has been explained, early in the microeconomic curriculum. Most A-level specifications then expect pupils to be able to explain, calculate and analyse the importance of income, price and cross-elasticity of demand. I slightly shift this sequencing: first teaching demand, supply and the price mechanism/equilibriums and only then explaining elasticity of demand.

The reason for this is that much of the impact of each relates to changes in the equilibrium price and quantity, so it can't be effectively explained without pupils understanding price determination. This also has the benefit of giving them more retrieval practice opportunities after the introduction of demand so that they achieve a certain amount of automaticity before attacking the more complex topic of elasticities.

In a 'Do now' quiz, I question pupils on the relationship between price and demand and what the income and substitute effect are to ensure pupils have the prerequisite knowledge and a broad enough schema to understand elasticity of demand.

Provided we're all ready, then I can return to my example of a can of Irn-Bru. Nobody is more loyal to Scotland's favourite drink, and by explaining that I would consume the same amount almost no matter how much it costs, I introduce the idea that brand loyalty means that some products see only a small change in demand when their price goes up. I introduce this as responsiveness to price.

Then as a non-example, I explain how goods with many similar substitutes like toilet paper would suffer a large reduction in demand from a price increase. Having presented an example and a non-example, I can now introduce the abstract concept of price elasticity of demand and ask pupils to complete practice questions on these. I then gradually introduce different influences on a good's price elasticity and pupils set pupils an extended writing task explaining each one and why it influences the price elasticity of demand of a particular good. Pupils explain why a particular good is likely to be relatively elastic or inelastic. And finally, we can discuss the concept of perfect elasticity of demand.

Only after this process – example, non-example, abstraction – do I introduce diagrams and require pupils to practice these extensively until they reach fluency. These can then be used to explain how elasticity impacts firms' profits, and indirect taxation can lead to increased tax revenues. Introducing case studies on the UK's sugar tax is a useful way of combining this with a diagrammatical analysis.

It is only when it is clear pupils have a comprehensive understanding of the concept that I would introduce the mathematical formula with a further extensive amount of pupil practice. And one final important point: it is important that the format of the questions changes; for example, by being worded differently to ensure pupils are having to think deeply about each problem.

CLASSICAL AND KEYNESIAN SUPPLY CURVES

A common critique from economists of the economics curriculum is that macroeconomics becomes a reductive 'Smith v Keynes' debate, and in fact it is a common feature of most macroeconomics model answers shown in examiners' reports. Despite the ubiquitous nature of these answers, pupils often still struggle to explain the difference between the classical and Keynesian understanding of aggregate supply. While most pupils can quickly learn to draw the different supply curves, it is understanding why they are different – and the impact this has on debates around government intervention – that often confuses pupils.

I start by teaching the classical supply curve and the notion of factor markets being in equilibrium in the long run. There is a useful opportunity to link this to microeconomics and what they have already learned on price determination and why excess demand and supply should not persist. I also like to introduce Say's Law at this point to explain why it was believed that supply creates its own demand. As well as making for some interesting hinterland knowledge**, it also becomes a useful way to compare demand-side management. After this, pupils practise explaining and drawing a classical long run aggregate supply curve. I then explain why increasing aggregate demand does not lead to higher real GDP. This is a useful opportunity for some spaced retrieval practice to see if pupils remember what the components of aggregate demand are and the factors that lead to changes in aggregate demand.

Here, I show a timeline of economic thought. Having explained Smith's and Say's views of self-correcting markets, I discuss the Great Depression and the persistent mass unemployment that led people to believe that the economy would not self-correct to a natural rate. The issue, they concluded, was not the capacity of the economy but a lack of demand. This is a useful chance to assess if pupils understand the concept of a classical long run aggregate supply model by asking them to explain why it should not persist.

** Say's Law states that the source of demand is production itself, because in order to buy something, an economic agent must first have sold – and therefore produced – something. It was first expressed by Jean-Baptiste Say in his 1803 work, *Treatise on Political Economy* and gave support to government non-intervention in markets, or laissez-faire economics.

The timeline enables pupils to understand how economic thought evolved and why new explanations were needed. And that's when I introduce the concept of demand-side management and Keynes' view of aggregate supply. If this is a new lesson, I start it by including questions about the marginal propensity to consume and consumer confidence in the 'Do now' quiz at the start so that pupils are refamiliarised with this prerequisite knowledge. Once I've explained this and pupils have answered questions to show they understand the difference between the Keynesian and classical models of aggregate supply, I introduce them to the Keynesian aggregate supply curve and we practise drawing it.

It's only really now that my pupils are ready to consider why shifts in aggregate demand can lead to economic growth in a Keynesian model when there is spare capacity. Fiscal stimulus policies in the UK after the financial crash are a useful way to show this and a nice way to introduce the topic of the financial crash in preparation for their later study of financial economics.

The final concept that is often overlooked is an understanding of why, at full capacity, the Keynesian and classical aggregate supply models have the same implications. It is important to be explicit about this to ensure pupils are not left with the common misconception that Keynes argued for permanently increasing government expenditure to boost economic growth.

As with any misconception between two related topics, I list 10 scenarios and ask pupils to confirm if they refer to the classical or Keynesian model of aggregate supply:

1. In the long run, the economy will be at its natural rate of output.
2. A lack of consumer confidence can lead to lower aggregate demand and prevent the economy from being at full capacity.
3. Increasing government spending will not impact unemployment or real GDP in the long run.
4. Supply will create its own demand.
5. Supply may not create its own demand if there is low consumer and business confidence.

6. The government has a role to create aggregate demand when the economy is at spare capacity.
7. Increased government spending will always lead to higher inflation.
8. The economy is always at full capacity in the long run.
9. The only focus for governments should be on increasing the productive capacity of the economy.
10. Increasing government expenditure will not increase real GDP when the economy is at full capacity.

The final question is a bit of a trick question to understand if pupils really understand the nuance of the Keynesian model of aggregate supply. This is because they should realise that this statement applies to both the Keynesian and classical aggregate supply curves as both models agree that increasing aggregate demand is ineffectual at the point where the economy is at full capacity. They only differ on the point that the economy is always at full capacity in the long run.

PUBLIC GOODS

Another deceptively simple concept is that of public goods. Deceptively, because there are three areas where the concept can be misunderstood: confusing public goods and the public sector; not appreciating the difference between a good being rivalrous and excludable; and misunderstanding why a government-run industry can prevent the free-rider problem from existing.

The best way to pre-empt the first misconception around the public sector and public goods in my experience is to start talking about goods being rivalrous and excludable before even mentioning that these are characteristics of public goods. By explaining what non-rivalrous means with examples and pupils completing questions on these, and doing the same with non-excludability, the result is that when I get to the point of defining a public good, I can clearly state that they are goods that are non-rivalrous and non-excludable and NOT goods provided by the government.

While teaching non-excludability, I explicitly ask pupils to explain how this differs from non-rivalry so that pupils can start to understand the difference between the two. This is then further established when asking pupils to explain exactly why goods are non-rivalrous and why they are non-excludable. A useful non-example to use here is healthcare. When pupils explain why this is not a public good, they demonstrate an understanding of what an economic definition of a public good is compared to a common understanding of the term.

The free-rider problem is usually relatively simple to explain and understand. I like to use a concrete example of a shared student flat where people wait for someone else to do the washing up and so ultimately it just doesn't get done. After all, it's likely to be a common experience for them all soon enough! This allows me to progress to conventional economic examples like flood defences and national defence. Where the confusion can come in is why these must be produced by the government. This can be overcome by a brief explanation of how the government can prevent free-riders by mandating payment through taxation. I then ask pupils to write a paragraph explaining why government-run firms avoid the free-rider problem to ensure this is fully understood.

FISCAL, MONETARY AND SUPPLY SIDE POLICY

When teaching different types of government policy, the confusion is often not in what each policy is but how they are different from each other and what the similarities are between them. After teaching each policy, I find this is actually quite easily resolved by the use of a hierarchical diagram to show the difference between them. Initially I look at whether a policy relates to increasing aggregate demand or supply. Then, I split aggregate demand into fiscal and monetary policy. This helps cement in pupils' minds the idea that these are alternative options with the same objective: to increase aggregate demand.

Then, under aggregate supply I show supply side policies. In fairness, the name is a bit of a giveaway. The important final part of this diagram though is the dotted line between supply side policy and fiscal policy to show how some interventionist fiscal policy like investing in transport infrastructure or education can impact both aggregate demand and long-run aggregate supply. It is important for pupils to appreciate this as it is often a useful evaluation point when considering whether a government should increase aggregate demand or the productive capacity of the economy. They could potentially do both. I find this model is also useful when pupils compare the advantages and disadvantages of each policy.

MONOPOLISTIC COMPETITION

Of all the different types of market structures, the one which often causes the most consternation is monopolistic competition. I suspect this is due to its hybrid nature and the increased complexity in drawing the diagram to represent it.

For me, the sequencing is important here. I start by teaching perfect competition, then monopoly and oligopoly and then finally monopolistic competition. This is because monopolistic competition has features in common with perfect competition and monopolies and so a strong understanding of preceding market structures makes this a far simpler topic to teach.

I use a hairdresser as a simple concrete example to explain how a firm can have many competitors and a low barrier to entry, yet also be subtly different to its competitors. What pupils need to understand is exactly why firms can influence the price by reducing their quantity (as each product is different and so reducing quantity increases scarcity and thus value) but also crucially why firms would not be able to maintain supernormal profits (low barrier to entry means that other firms would have an incentive to enter the market and drive the price down until it equalled average cost). After explaining these, I find specific questions asking pupils to explain this can assess adequately assess whether they fully understand it:

1. What characteristics of monopolistic competition are the same as perfect competition?
2. If there are many competitors, why are firms price makers?
3. What characteristic of monopolistic competition means that firms cannot make supernormal profits in the long run?
4. Explain what would happen if a firm in a monopolistically competitive market was making a supernormal profit.

5. At what point is a normal profit made?

The final step is to introduce the diagram. I start with the points that pupils are familiar with – downward sloping average and marginal revenue curves (asking pupils why this would be the case for monopolistic competition) and the 'Nike tick' marginal cost curve. Finally, I draw the average cost curve, emphasising the need for this to be tangential to the average revenue curve.

There is no getting away from the fact that it is a challenging diagram and an easy one to get wrong. The only solution is constant practice until pupils achieve fluency.

CONCLUSION

I hope reading this book has given you some food for thought that can help you refine your own economics lessons. So much of what I have learned has been in conversations with other wonderful teachers. My hope is that this can be a part of that conversation, and certainly not its final word.

For economics teaching to be research-informed, we need to understand what the research tells us are the best bets for successful pupil learning and discuss how this can best be implemented in our subject-specific context. This requires a dual approach of reading from teachers and researchers in other areas of the curriculum, while also creating a space where we can discuss implementation among ourselves as economics teachers.

It is only by continuing to keep abreast of what we know about excellent teaching and sharing how we are trying to implement it in economics lessons that we can overcome the deficits of having so few colleagues to collaborate with. Having said that, I am immensely grateful for the professional community we do have, and I would like to thank the economics teachers up and down the country who I have learned so much from. Much of what I have written has been a product of that learning.

In this regard, Twitter has been a godsend. While the economics teacher community online is small, it is filled with people who are incredibly generous with their time. Economics has a reputation as the 'dismal science', but there is no greater refutation of homo economicus as a self-interested being than the group of economics teachers collaborating online to better the teaching of our subject for the benefit of all our pupils.

I can't think of a greater privilege than to teach economics to a new generation (hopefully a few of whom will eventually teach it themselves). I hope this book contributes towards making that easier for some and that together we can continue to improve even further.

So, if you have any opinions on what I have said, then I would love to hear about them. I am most easily contactable on twitter @yousufhamid, and I relish the opportunity to continue the conversation with you.